52 THINKS

52 THINKS
Copyright © 2021 by Phillip T. Hopersberger

No part of this book may be reproduced in any form without the permission in writing form the author,
except for brief quotations for reviews or articles.

All rights reserved.

Cover Design:
Peter Ashford Hopersberger

Website:
www.TotallyWriteousCopy.com

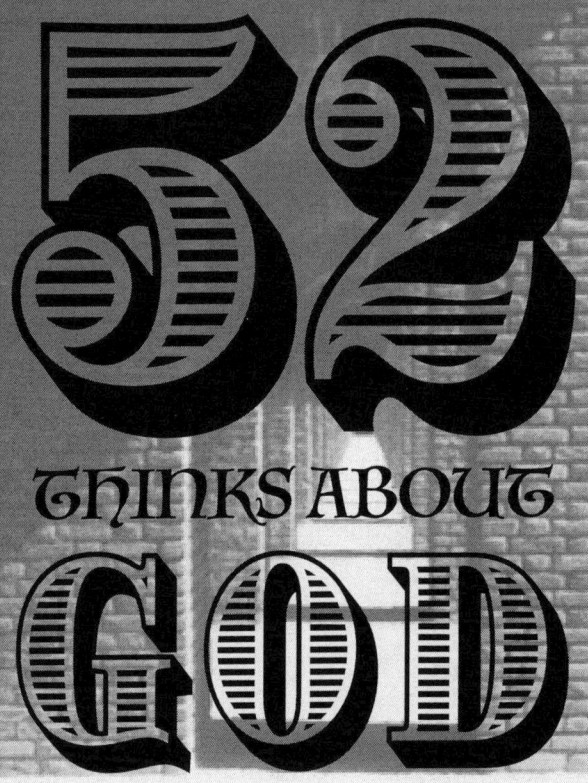

52 Thinks About God

Two-Minute Reads Each Week
for the Whole Year About God

A DEVOTIONAL BY

PHILLIP T. HOPERSBERGER

PUBLISHED BY
SHAKESPEARE'S IN THE ALLEY

In memory of Mary Esther and Joseph William...the best parents who always said, "You should be a writer!"

and

Charles John Huffam Dickens who might have been the best storywriter ever.

Mr. Beaver said, "Aslan is a lion – the Lion, the great Lion."

"Ooh," said Susan. "I'd thought he was a man. Is he quite safe? I shall feel rather nervous about meeting a lion."

"Safe?" said Mr. Beaver. "Who said anything about safe? 'Course he isn't safe. But he's good. He's the King, I tell you. He's wild, you know. Not like a tame lion."

– C.S. Lewis, *Chronicles of Narnia*

Introduction

Words create trails in the mind for thoughts to follow.

Good words lead down good paths. Bad words lead down bad paths. I have enjoyed the words of Phil Hopersberger for over a decade now—and Phil has consistently led my mind down good paths. I should warn you, though…Phil's words require courage to read.

He's got a way of colliding with the soul, provoking new thinking, contentiously anticipating wrong thinking—and unabashedly prodding us toward right thinking. Phil is my dear friend. He's got a way of making me feel better about myself with encouraging words and new ways of thinking that leave me more optimistic and hopeful. If you want to think better and live better, Phil is your friend, too, and this book has a good chance of taking you down the best path you've ever been down.

If you are a courageous reader and a lover of the truth, *52 Thinks* is for you. Beneath Phil's words I've consistently experienced from him powerful love and grace. Knowing that has helped me listen to Phil and to trust him. You can trust his heart and you can trust his words.

Phil wields words well—so well that I've hired him to write for me time after time. When I had to choose a wordsmith to experience the Holy Land and then write 104 articles for me, Phil was the one I chose. And he sure delivered. He made me look good and I'm so glad I chose him. I hope you'll choose to read this book and take it to heart.

I think the thinks Phil will help you "thunk" will make you glad you dove into *52 Thinks*. Happy trails!

Ron Forseth

Author, *The Wisdom Challenge*
Founder, *The Wisdom Society*
Owner, Forseth Development, Inc.

From the Author

Every Christmas Eve, our family would huddle around the television to watch George C. Scott in our favorite rendition of Charles Dickens' *A Christmas Carol*. Our children are grown and gone now, but they still watch it every Christmas Eve (I gave them a copy when they left home).

We've done that now for over 25 years, and the story never gets old. Why would a short story written in 1843 still matter? Because it is a story well told, and redemption is always relevant, even today. And it's not just important on Christmas. Reclamation is important every day.

Which is why I wrote *52 Thinks*, the culmination of years of newspaper columns that I penned for those who are not Christians, for the person who is searching for truth, for God, and Jesus. This is for genuine seekers.

Not every column is about Christmas, actually only a few, as they were originally written throughout each year, but as Dickens wrote, we are all on the same journey. It is that spirit of Christmas that is the theme because we all have the same questions about life.

Why am I here? Is God real? Can I know Him? Is the Bible His inspired message to us? What happens when I die? What's my purpose in life?

If you've been looking for answers, then *52 Thinks* is for you. I hope it helps you get some answers and to meet the God of the Bible, who promised this to all seekers who really want to know Him:

"Then you will call upon Me and come and pray to Me, and I will listen to you. And you will seek Me and find Me, when you search for Me with all your heart (Jeremiah 29:12-13)."

52 Thinks is for you, and for everyone else who is seeking the God of the Bible. He promises you that you will find Him if you really want to know Him, with all your heart. My prayer is that you do. He's more than worth it!

Week 1: Be Like Scrooge!

"Darkness is cheap, and Scrooge liked it."

Like Charlie Brown, the true meaning of Christmas evades some folks every twenty-fifth of December.

Fortunately, another Charlie peeled back some of the mystery with his classic 1843 tale, *A Christmas Carol*. Although most rely on the film versions, instead of reading Charles Dickens' masterpiece— a measly 29,000 words that can be read in just two-hours— *A Christmas Carol* can be reduced even more to only one word… repent.

Repent is a religious word that means to change your mind, or your direction (I repented of going home and went back to work). For Scrooge, he decides to change his stingy and selfish life, and to embrace Christmas, something his nephew Fred sums up nicely:

"I have always thought of Christmas as a good time: a kind, forgiving, charitable, pleasant time: the only time I know of, in the long calendar of the year, when men and women seem by one consent to open their shut-up hearts freely, and to think of people below them as if they really were fellow-passengers to the grave, and not another race of creatures bound on other journeys."

Note these literary nuggets, *"shut-up hearts"* and *"fellow-passengers to the grave."* Dickens turned a phrase as easily as a doorknob, or a Marley encrusted doorknocker, and understood human nature like no other author. His scalpel-like words can even reveal our own Scrooged-up hearts (*"Mankind was my business," Marley moaned*).

If your heart is "shut-up" at this festive time, and don't "get" Christmas, consider Phillips Brooks' famous carol's line, *"Where meek souls will receive Him still, the dear Christ enters in."* Meek

is another religious word that has the idea of a wild horse that is now broken, gentle, and easily led.

Brooks was influenced by the Apostle John who said, *"He was in the world, and the world was made through Him, and the world did not know Him. He came to His own, and those who were His own did not receive Him. But as many as received Him, to them He gave the right to become children of God, even to those who believe in His name, who were born, not of blood nor of the will of the flesh nor of the will of man, but of God (John 1:10-13)."*

The real meaning of Christmas is revealed when the One Who created everything literally enters your heart because you receive Him, just like a Christmas present. You have to be born of God through His Spirit. Jesus made that clear when He said, *"Truly, truly, I say to you, unless one is born again he cannot see the kingdom of God (John 3:3)."*

Christmas only makes sense if the Author of Christmas, *"now in flesh appearing,"* comes inside of you because like Scrooge, you repented and with meekness let Him lead you in a new direction.

That was Jesus' very first sermon, repent and believe (Mark 1:15). And as Linus said, *"That's what Christmas is all about, Charlie Brown."* So, be like Scrooge…repent, and believe, and have a Merry Christmas!

Week 2:
Bara

"...who calls into being that which does not exist (Romans 4:17)."

As a screenwriter, I "call into being that which does not exist" daily.

Every story begins with a blank page, which made me wonder about the all-time bestseller and how much of it you've seriously read. Surprisingly, most have read less than 10 percent of the Bible.

Despite corroboration by Archaeology, History, prophetic predictions (now past proofs), multiple eyewitness accounts, and staying intact and accurate for over 34 centuries, many scoff at its claim to be supernaturally written by chosen men, moved by God's Spirit.

You could argue against all of that, but you can't contest that this book is unique and has changed millions of lives. I've experienced this change, what Jesus called being born again by God's Spirit (John 3:3).

That was over 40 years ago when His Spirit entered my body and started transforming me with His living words. As a writer, I've even had glimpses of this Creator-inspiration that the Bible's authors experienced.

My innate gift with words has always been with me. At a Parent-Teacher Conference, my 7th grade teacher told my Mother that my papers were so good that she thought my older brothers were writing them, so she cancelled her lesson-plan one day and made all of us write a paper at our desks…just to catch me!

My Mother was offended until she told her that she witnessed me write the best paper she'd ever read. My Mother was beaming when she got home and told me all of this.

I cannot take credit for this God-given gift and as I said, have had a sense of what the Bible's authors felt when I write. Nothing mystical

or weird, and not on the same level of their inspiration, but definitely a clear sense of His leading me with crazy good story tie-ins, cute plot twists, unintended structure, and clever dialogue.

It's wild, and sometimes I just look up and laugh because I know it wasn't my idea at all. It's Him with me on the keyboard.

Each time I look at a blank page that becomes a 120-page script, well, that's God the Spirit who's truly responsible for that. A Hebrew word, *bara*, fits this act of creation. It's used only a few times in the Old Testament, and it means "to create something out of nothing," like a seed "emerging" from the ground that bears fruit. Something (a pear tree with roots, leaves and pears) comes out of nothing (a tiny hard seed).

Granted, famous writers who are not Christians have penned great stuff, much better than me, but all creativity comes from our Creator (even if they take the credit). It's similar to John chapter 12, when God the Father spoke to God the Son, and some in the crowd only heard thunder. Do you recognize God's voice in your life or do you just hear rumbles of thunder? The Bible says that this kind of intimacy is possible because of Jesus.

Jesus made a way back to God for us, the spiritually dead, when He died on the cross and rose again. He is this living Word (John 1:1-14), will "*bara*" a new you, and *"give life to the dead* (Romans 4:17)." An imperishable seed, the living and abiding Word of God, can be inside of you (1 Peter 1:23), and call into being a new life that doesn't exist…yet.

Week 3:
Forewarned is Forearmed

"The greatest danger occurs at the moment of victory."
- Napoleon

The hardest man to rescue is the one who thinks he's safe.

We've all seen that ending in a movie. Oblivious to the danger (but we see it coming), they lose it all because they think they're safe, lulled into a false sense of security.

Convinced of victory, as Napoleon warns, they lose. If you think you're safe, read no further. But…if you want assurance for that happy Hollywood ending, then consider these four spiritual warnings.

- You think you're safe because of your religion. *"Unless one is born again, he cannot see the Kingdom of God* (John 3:1-15)." Jesus gave only one requirement that had nothing to do with denominations. Jesus told Nicodemus, the religious expert with the "right" religion, that you must be born again. He did not say be Jewish, Catholic, or Protestant. He said you must be born again. So what is born again exactly?

We are born physically, but cursed with a spiritual cancer called Sin. Sin is fatal (we die) and it is only radiated if you are made again, recreated by a second spiritual birth, when you choose to let Him come inside your body. He will only invade upon invitation, if you vacate the throne in your heart, which is repentance (you acknowledge your sin, your helplessness, and give up your will to Him). If not, then the second death is your ending, which is your choice too, to pay for your sins yourself (Hell). His love is never forced.

- You think you're safe because you're not that bad. *"If you keep the whole Law, and break just one commandment, you are guilty of all* (James 2:10)." If you are trusting in you…your efforts, your religion, your denomination, your ancestry, then Jesus died for

nothing (Galatians 2:21). God's standard is perfection, not just being good enough because just one sin means you're guilty of all, imperfect. You trying is impossible because you are a spiritual corpse, dead in your un-radiated sin (Ephesians 2:1).

- You think you're safe because you believe. *"Even the demons believe and tremble* (James 2:19)." The demons saw Him, so what's the difference in your faith and their faith? They are not going to Heaven. If your belief is not a saving, eternal faith, and just head knowledge, an intellectual assent, then you're not safe. Believing is not trusting. You can believe a rickety old bridge over a canyon will hold you up, but running out on it is genuine trust.

- You think you're safe because you asked for forgiveness. Forgiveness does not happen because you ask for it. Forgiveness is on His terms. You must come to Him broken; sorry, and admitting your good works are useless. Ask Him to come inside and save you because of His sacrifice in your place (John 1:12-13). Four warnings and forewarned.

A happy ending is assured to all who give up (John 5:24). Surrender your crown to the One who loved you so much, He died in your place. Be saved or be safe.

Week 4: But I Think

"I the Lord do not change...(Malachi 3:6)."

The mirror tells me I have changed; sometimes it shouts.

Time affects everything, except God.

We call this attribute Immutability, and it's linked to His revealing Himself to us in a stunning Creation (Romans 1:20), His Word (Matthew 5:18), and the Incarnation–when our Creator became flesh and blood as Jesus of Nazareth (John 1:1-4; Hebrews 13:8).

The weight of our differences from Him is not only that we change, but our opinions that are based on capricious authorities and influences fluctuate too, which affects how we see God's truth, or even care to. When discussing spiritual things, most folks have lots of opinions, so I like to ask, *"What do you base that on?"*

Invariably it's, *"But I think...."*

We, the fallible, become the authority, but honestly...can you trust yourself?

Truth varies with cultures. Ancient Rome and Greece allowed sex with children and goats, Aztecs ate their heartless human sacrifices, Canaanites burnt babies, and scientists err (Copernicus critics, bleeding as a cure, Lister and sterile surgeries, Darwin's theory as fact, or Pluto as our ninth planet).

Truth and authority are in flux because we are always changing. Always.

So what you base your opinion on, especially in spiritual matters, matters a great deal. God (Jesus) should not be based on opinion. So God gave us an absolute true north; an immutable authority that confirms what is objective, unchanging Truth, the Bible.

John's Gospel, chapters 18-19, discusses this truth and authority. Pontius Pilate, Rome's authority in Jerusalem, asked Jesus, *"What is truth?"* Later, Jesus told Pilate, *"You would have no authority over Me unless it had been given to you from above."* These were critical moments that revealed God's absolute Truth, and the Authority behind it.

Your eternal destiny should not dangle on the thread of an opinion, but you can be sure, and have "true north" on this journey and not get lost, forever (1 John 5:13). Is the Bible supernatural, God-inspired words to know Him? Was Jesus God? Did He rise from the dead to prove these claims? Why won't being good make you righteous (just knowing, without repentance, is not a saving faith, James 2:19)? The Bible explains all of this.

A friend told me, *"My philosophy is to do good to people."* I replied, *"That's great, but what about your sins?"*

The Bible says that goodness won't save you (James 2:10). For God to be unchanging, He cannot ignore sin and must stay righteous in His Immutability (or He'd be like a bribed judge). So, He provided Himself, became sin to save us, and took the judgment we deserved. Love and Justice met at the cross (2 Corinthians 5:21).

Truth came into History and conquered Death as proof of His absolute Authority. Jesus ended "but I think" opinions when He said, "*I am the way, and the truth, and the life; no man comes to the Father, but through Me* (John 14:6)." Or maybe Jesus lied, but I'm human, been wrong before, so I'll take His Immutability over what I think, every time.

Week 5: Butchy

"'...But who do you say that I am?' And Simon Peter answered and said, 'Thou art the Christ... (Matthew 16:15-16).'"

Time out! All five of us kids flopped onto the curb, exhausted.

Some of the best two-hand-touch football games were played on my street in Detroit, and Butchy led us.

Butchy was older, so he was always the official quarterback for both teams. We all looked up to him. One of those guys you never forget; he made you feel like a million bucks. When Butchy chose to throw to you it made you feel special. You dare not drop it.

After some huffing and puffing, Butchy asked one of those playground questions kids ask like if you had three wishes or won a million bucks…*"Who would you want to meet if you went back in time?"*

As if possible, we deliberated it with great seriousness. For 1971, our answers were predictable. Jeff chose Daniel Boone. Skinny Doogan picked Washington. Ray grabbed Lincoln, and that left me. The pressure was on, but I knew that the greatest "baseball card" to collect as a ten-year-old had to be Jesus.

Looking back, it just seemed like He was the one guy you'd want to meet above anybody else. This had nothing to do with theology. Even then I knew Jesus would be a wow-factor guy. He had all the answers, did miracles, and even rose from the dead!

That sunny Detroit day is still clear to me 50 years later, and sometime in the next 50 I'll get my wish.

According to the Bible, seeing Him is a sure thing, as is meeting other famous Christians like Washington, Lincoln, and even the

Apostle Peter…who saw Jesus, and heard Him ask that 'who am I' question in person!

Wanna' know a secret? You're going to see Him too, eyeball to eyeball. *"For we must all appear before the judgment seat of Christ, that each one may be recompensed for his deeds in the body, according to what he has done, whether good or bad (2 Corinthians 5:10)."*

So here's my question, are you ready to meet Jesus?

I hope so, and I'm also hoping to see my buddies in Heaven too, especially Butchy. It's not a fair comparison, but the way he made me feel is like Jesus does now…genuinely accepted, pretty darn special, and included right along with stars like Peter.

Peter's answer is a classic because he caught that Jesus was God, in the flesh! Jesus threw a deep pass and Peter made a spectacular reception. Imagine his euphoria when Jesus looked at him in that recognition moment, and then consider what he felt later on when he denied his best friend…three times.

Did you know Peter was so near that Jesus heard him? *"And the Lord turned and looked at Peter (Luke 22:61)."* Despite that rejection Jesus forgave Peter, and He can forgive you too. I hope you receive His pass before that day when He turns to look at you (John 1:12). You'd make a great catch.

# Week 6:
The 90 (Minute) Psalm

> "But do not let this one fact escape your notice, beloved, that with the Lord one day is as a thousand years, and a thousand years as one day (2 Peter 3:8)."

What if…I told you it's 9 o'clock and by 10:30 you'll be dead?

How would you spend your 90 minutes, and what would really matter? This is the gist of Peter's life-changing verse above.

Peter's quoting Moses who wrote Psalm 90, the oldest Psalm in the Old Testament, and warning us not to miss this one fact…in light of eternity, from where God views time (and us), our life is only about 90 minutes long. Peter says this is a fact, and if true then King David ruled Israel three days ago (1,000 BC) and Jesus has only been gone for a weekend (33 AD).

The biblical math from eternity's perspective is that a day equals 1,000 years so living to 100 is about two hours. Psalm 90:10 says that 70 is average, but 80 if we're healthy, so let's say for simplicity's sake that with modern medicine you live to be 90. The math is personally unnerving since I'll be 60 next March, so my 90 minutes is down to around half an hour or so on Earth.

And I'm excited about that! Why?

In light of 90 minutes, it's ironic, even stupid, that we fret about money, careers, mortgages, debt, possessions, health, diets, inheritances, retirement, and death. If you believed Moses and Peter, and you thought you only had 90 minutes, minus your current age, how would you spend those precious minutes here with Jesus waiting to meet you there?

Albert Einstein, a math genius, said of Time (foolishly), *"I never think of the future, it comes soon enough."* His 90 minutes were only 76 minutes (he died in 1955). The Bible tells us to think about

the future because we're all headed there, and at the end of Time Jesus is there...alive, risen from the dead, and waiting as Friend or Judge. You'll see Him soon, in just a few minutes, so choose wisely how you use your remaining clock ticks.

Jesus loves you and what you do with His death on the cross for your sin determines your relationship to Him, both now and at minute 91. If you are not sure about Heaven, 100 percent positive that you'll be greeted as a friend after your 90 minutes, you can be sure (1 John 5:11-13). You can make your peace now by receiving Him (John 1:12), and extend your 90 minutes...forever.

Just give up; admit your sin, genuinely turn from it, and ask Jesus to forgive you (Romans 10:9). It's simple, but serious. This is a life-changing verse because it's an eternity-changing fact. You have scant minutes to decide if it's true because your life is just a smoky wisp. I hope you won't *"let this one fact escape your notice,"* and that you're as excited to see Jesus in 5,400 seconds as I am, as Lord, Savior, and Friend.

Week 7:
October is Coming

"He found nothing but leaves (Mark 11:13)."

October is a long way off, but I love that season because our apple trees make the best applesauce. I protect those apples all year, but once the trees are picked I ignore them, and so do the pesky animals because now they have no real value.

Mark can relate.

Mark's record here in chapter 11 is one of the two times that Jesus destroyed something in nature (the other was the demons He cast out into a herd of pigs that ran over a cliff). This fig tree had no fruit, *"nothing but leaves,"* and He cursed it. Seems extreme, but it was symbolic of what He had found in Israel…no spiritual fruit on the tree of Israel.

With days before His death and the New Covenant, Jesus was done with their lip service (Mark 7:6), and wanted a heart change that He did not find (Mark's next section is the second time He threw out the moneychangers from the Temple, which Israel's leaders had turned from a worship center into big profits). They had drifted too far from God.

Religious hypocrites are nothing new. Good riddance to fakers with green leaves and no real value, but it's also a good reminder… one day Jesus will inspect your life for fruit too. *"For we must all appear before the judgment seat of Christ* (2 Corinthians 5:10)."

Not "fruit" like being good or going to church (Isaiah 64:6, Titus 3:5), but real repentance as Jesus' baptizing cousin said in Matthew 3:8, *"bring forth fruit in keeping with repentance."* He wants a change of heart, a surrender of your rebellious attitude of indifference to your sin and His love for you. Jesus wants you back, but your sin separates you from God (Isaiah 59:2).

So who cares about fruit and repentance?

Well, you should care because you are going to meet Jesus and He won't care a fig about church or being good. His standard is perfection, absolute holiness, and the absence of sin (Habakkuk 1:13, Matthew 5:48). It makes sense since Heaven has no sin, but no one is that pure, so is it even possible?

"Nobody's perfect, and He can't really expect me to be holy? If I'm honest, I've lied, cheated, stolen, lusted, and busted just about every commandment in thought, word, or deed. So if He wants to have an impossible standard, I don't care. I'm guilty, so be it, and if I'm honest, not really very good either...if 'good' means holy, then I'm lost."

God knew our broken-helplessness, His responsibility to be just and punish lawbreakers, and so He provided Himself...a lamb. Only God can meet His holy standard, and that's why God became a man. That's Christmas and Easter.

Jesus, the sinless man, was that perfect payment for us. God loved us, reconciled us, and remained just by having His Son die in our place. His sacrifice made us as righteous as God (2 Corinthians 5:21). This good news is free, but you must choose it. Fall seems a long way off, but October is coming (Hebrews 9:27).

Week 8: 155,000

"...to die is gain (Philippians 1:21)."

That's the number of people who died today.

A sobering statistic, and worth repeating to let the enormity of it soak in…155,000 people died this very day (just imagine if Grand Rapids, Michigan emptied overnight).

It made me wonder how many people die each day after my neighbor had a massive heart attack and suddenly died! We were shocked and saddened, especially since as far as we knew he never let Jesus be his master. I invited him to church once and he declined saying, *"The walls would fall down."*

Another friend just got diagnosed with ovarian cancer and will be part of that 155,000 soon. Luckily, she accepted Jesus in 1981 and can't wait to see Him. As I prayed for her healing, I wondered what Jesus wanted for her. Was it really better to stay here in a broken world, healed, or as Paul said, *"to die is gain."* Wouldn't Jesus rather have her in unimaginable bliss, as soon as possible, to shower her with the blessings He's planned for centuries?

When I thought on that, I had a massive paradigm shift.

For her and Jesus, death will be a precious introduction of inexpressible joy as they exchange first smiles. What a moment!

Considering her death from His viewpoint, wanting her home, changed my prayers for her. So if we are 100% sure that Jesus will welcome us as His precious possession, as she is convinced of—and not in fear as one who's rejected His salvation—then death is an incredible gain! This changes everything! But can you be that confident, and really know for sure?

The Apostle John said that that was precisely why the Bible was written. *"These things I have written to you who believe in the*

name of the Son of God, so that you may know that you have eternal life (1 John 5:13)." So if Heaven can be a certainty, and is so much better, why not take her home yesterday?

Peter answers, *"The Lord is not slow about His promise, as some count slowness, but is patient toward you, not wishing for any to perish but for all to come to repentance* (2 Peter 3:9)." His followers remain here as a compass pointing to True North, Jesus. Unfortunately, most of the 56 million people who will die this year, like my neighbor, will politely ignore Jesus, just as He said:

"Enter through the narrow gate; for the gate is wide and the way is broad that leads to destruction, and there are many who enter through it. For the gate is small and the way is narrow that leads to life, and there are few who find it (Matthew 7:13-14)."

So…are you in today's 155,000? I'm sure my neighbor didn't think so. Today may be your last chance, so why risk that when you can know for sure (Luke 12:20)? The Lord waits patiently, but He won't wait forever. Why not make today what He wants for you…a real gain changer (2 Corinthians 6:2)?

Week 9: Precious

"Lead on! The night is waning fast, and it is precious time to me."

So says a now fully aware Ebenezer Scrooge to his last visitor, a Grim Reaper apparition who is unmistakably Death himself. Like a masked executioner, Scrooge pleads with him to be quick, and calls his dwindling time "precious."

Precious isn't used much now, but a fitting description as the currency slipping through his stingy fingers is the only commodity Death trades in – Time. Do not miss Dickens' meaning. This Phantom is taking a life, and specifically, Scrooge is tonight's transaction.

Charles Dickens' *A Christmas Carol* is, word for word, the one holiday story you should read before you die. It is brilliantly brief, but do not mistake his lean writing for folly…it is timeless, pregnant with genius, and his reclamation tale takes only two hours to read!

So, what exactly is precious…to you?

Think hard on that. Decide what is your most precious thing, and then consider how to safeguard it. If you're honest you'll see it can only be Time, and like Scrooge you are losing it…right now, this very minute slips away.

And what would God (who is outside of Time) consider precious? He says our faith in Jesus and His dripping blood (1 Peter 1:7 and 19), His promises (2 Peter 1:4), His love (Psalm 36:7), and the death of his godly ones (Psalm 116:15). These all fit hand and glove into Dickens' choice, and bring to mind two other precious-conscious writers.

In Tolkien's *The Lord of the Rings*, Gollum calls his magic Ring "Precious," and its power transforms his desire into deadly lust and corrupts him. Sin changes him into a horrific monster, as it does to us. Thankfully, Tolkien's friend, C.S. Lewis persuaded the doubtful

author to publish his Hobbit tale, and then Lewis wrote of another "Precious."

"It is a serious thing to live in a society of possible gods and goddesses, to remember that the dullest most uninteresting person you can talk to may one day be a creature which, if you saw it now, you would be strongly tempted to worship, or else a horror and a corruption such as you now meet, if at all, only in a nightmare. All day long we are, in some degree helping each other to one or the other of these destinations. It is in light of these overwhelming possibilities, it is with the awe and the circumspection proper to them, that we should conduct all of our dealings with one another, all friendships, all loves, all play, all politics. There are no ordinary people. You have never talked to a mere mortal. Nations, cultures, arts, and civilizations–these are mortal, and their life is to ours as the life of a gnat. But it is immortals whom we joke with, work with, marry, snub, and exploit–immortal horrors or everlasting splendors." Souls are precious too.

Dickens got it right. Time is precious, and the holidays remind us of that, but Lewis reminds us that only Jesus can help us get more Time, through faith in His precious blood sacrifice you get life eternal. And that's what *Ebenezer* means in Hebrew, Stone of Help, a very precious stone.

Week 10: Belly Button Theology

"And there is salvation in no one else; for there is no other name under Heaven that has been given among men by which we must be saved (Acts 4:12)."

Cassius Clay said, *"It's not bragging if you can back it up."*

Truth tends to be that way. Exclusive. Your address is the same, two plus two equals four, north on a compass, a switch is on or off, and Jesus is the only way to Heaven (He said that, not me). I hear the brakes grinding to a halt on that one, but you knew it was coming. Jesus is exclusive.

Before I became a Christian I figured there was one God and multiple ways to get to Him, like trails going up a mountain. All of them lead to the same peak. I was wrong. Jesus squelched that when He said, *"I am the way, the truth, and the life. No man comes to the Father but through Me (John 14:6)."* You're wrong too if you have my peak theology (only a friend tells you that you have broccoli in your teeth).

Our sense of fair play and justice screams this is wrong, arrogant, and intolerant, which it totally is…IF…it's not true.

But…IF…it is true, that Jesus is God and proved it by rising from the dead, then it's prolly a good idea to listen to Him because He "can back it up." Another thing that's exclusive is that there is only one way out of this world into the next. We will all die. So what does this have to do with your umbilicus (belly button)?

All of us have a navel, but whether it's an "innie" or an "outie" is a matter of chance. Most of us have an innie, about 96%, which is a similar division to what Jesus said in Matthew 7:13-14, *"The way is narrow that leads to life and few are those who find it."* Most of you will be the 96% and ignore this truth because *"Broad is the way that leads to destruction and many are those who enter by it."*

For Jesus to make these claims is exclusively exclusive, as truth always is, which is the "innie" theology…you must be "in" Christ. That means repent of your selfish ways and sin, and surrender to Him to be your Master, and believe that God raised Him from dead to pay for your sin, and ask Him "in" to your heart (John 1:12).

Although Jesus is exclusive in His claims for salvation (disqualifying all other religions), the "outie" part is that it is an "outward" invitation to all. It's not a private club. All are welcome. All can come to the cross. The invitation to be saved is proclaimed to the entire world. *"For God so loved the world…* (John 3:16)."

An empty grave backed it up; so it's not arrogant to claim to be the only way to get to Heaven. It's like saying your belly button is arrogant for being so exclusive. There can be only one…umbilicus.

Week 11:
Seven

"Have I not seen Jesus our Lord? (1 Corinthians 9:1)."

"All of a sudden a shot rang out…and someone screamed. I saw him slumped forward in his seat."

An eyewitness is invaluable for proof, especially when that eyewitness is part of an historic murder. On February 9, 1956, Samuel Seymour was 96 years old when he appeared on the television show, "I've Got A Secret." He was just such a witness.

Five-year-old Seymour went to the theater in Washington, D.C. on April 14th and saw Abraham Lincoln murdered by John Wilkes Booth. The last surviving eyewitness to this tragedy, he sat in the balcony across from the Presidential Box and saw Lincoln arrive, waving and smiling. Can you imagine?

After the shot rang out, he was confused by all the commotion and concerned about Booth who tumbled *"over the balcony rail and landed on the stage."* What luck to be there to see history, albeit horrible, but…imagine if…Lincoln came back to life and spoke to Seymour! Would you still believe his story or think he's a liar?

Saul of Tarsus, also known as Paul the Apostle, did just that when he met and talked with a murdered Jew from Nazareth (Acts 9). Paul was an expert teacher on Judaism, and before this remarkable encounter, he imprisoned Jews and murdered them for saying Jesus was alive and their Messiah.

Consider how Paul's encounter with a dead man transformed his life's direction, and if you'd do this for a lie:

• He lost everything, endured hardships, ridicule, beatings, stoning, and imprisonments.

• He told everyone he met, and traveled everywhere to do so, even getting shipwrecked.

• He was so convincing that thousands gave up their lives (literally) on his testimony.

• He started churches that made Christianity a worldwide force that affected billions.

• He wrote most of the New Testament so we could scrutinize his claims about Jesus.

• He gave his head to a Roman executioner for what he believed to be unequivocally true.

He lost everything on purpose; only a genuine "dead" Jesus encounter warrants that radical a change.

Mr. Seymour died two months after his television appearance, but if he had claimed to see Lincoln alive, several months later, and knew it was a lie, when threatened with death to tell the truth, he'd have recanted. A man will die for a cause he believes in, but nobody would die for what they knew was a lie. Paul gladly died for it.

I was born in 1961 so I rely on these eyewitnesses, the former can be seen on *YouTube*, but Paul's account must be read in the New Testament. Both accounts are considered to be historically sound as primary sources. If you take the time to read Paul's letters and decide he's a liar, then you've wasted a few days. But if you don't, and he's truthful, then Paul's seven words will cost you everything, forever. Why not check out what he said he saw. Seven could be your lucky number, and you know what rhymes with seven?

Week 12:
Exit, Exit...Flee All About It!

"Jesus said to him, 'I am the way, and the truth, and the life. No man comes to the Father, but through Me (John 14:6).'"

I was in London recently and noticed something strange while riding on the Tube (the local subway). It struck me how almost everyone was reading a newspaper!

I worked for a newspaper for several years, so this intrigued me since no one really does this in America anymore. Nowadays, we get our headlines instantly on our phones or cable news networks.

Another difference was the Tube stops along the line, like Piccadilly Circus or Notting Hill Gate, because "WAY OUT" marks the stairs to the street above. Most of us rarely notice the red EXIT sign above a door, unless there's an emergency like a fire or an earthquake, so WAY OUT was pretty unique. I mean on the flight over they make a point of directing your attention to the EXIT door, but most of us ignore EXIT signs, right? But WAY OUT...no one misses that!

Biblically speaking, Jesus is the only EXIT door. He said He was "the way (out)." Note that He claimed exclusivity...to be the only way, the only truth, and the only life. He disqualified every other religion with those words, or He was a liar (His recorded life in the New Testament would eliminate that possibility, as would insanity to make such a bold claim).

We will all exit this world, and it may be without warning. I had a cousin die suddenly last week. He visited his brother, played golf, went out to dinner, and then died in his sleep. We were all shocked, and deeply grieved! No one saw his exit coming.

The Bible says if you exit without Jesus what is on the other side will be much worse than just death (Revelation 20:11-15). In John chapter 10, Jesus told some religious big shots that being good

didn't matter and neither did their religion. You have to go through Him, God in human form, and He even called Himself the Door:

"So Jesus said to them again, 'Truly, truly, I say to you, I am the door of the sheep. All who came before Me are thieves and robbers, but the sheep did not hear them. I am the door; if anyone enters through Me, he will be saved, and will go in and out and find pasture. The thief comes only to steal and kill and destroy; I came that they may have life, and have it abundantly.'"

Years ago, when there was a big headline event paperboys hawked the special edition on street corners with the refrain, *"Extra, Extra, read all about it!"* Today, Jesus is that big news story and those red EXIT signs you see every day are your warning that you're going to exit this world. They are also a reminder that Jesus is your only WAY OUT. You can't be good enough, and religion won't save you, so maybe open the door of your heart (Revelation 3:20). He is the good news we all need to hear these days.

Week 13:
E-logical E-zekiel 18

"...to set free those who were doomed to death (Psalm 102:20)."

I love the new AT&T commercials *"when just ok is not ok,"* especially the one with Dr. Francis and his new surgery patient. The patient's wife asks the nurse in his room if she's ever worked with him and she says, *"Oh yeah...he's okay."* (Just okay?)

Dr. Francis appears in the doorway and unprofessionally yells down the hall, *"Guess who just got re-instated!"* Once he's inside the room, he quietly admits, *"Well, not officially."* Then he asks the now visibly worried patient if he's nervous about his surgery. (Yes!)

"Yeah, me too. Don't worry about it. We'll figure it out." As he abruptly leaves, the cavalier doctor tosses this over his shoulder, *"I'll see ya' in there."* (Say what?)

This patient is doomed and we laugh, but if it were real it'd be scary bad. Now suppose God had a commercial jingle, it might be, *"when just good is not good enough."* Why? If you're trusting in your good works to make you acceptable to a holy God, then you're doomed (and actually insulting Jesus).

Consider Ezekiel chapter 18 and verse 20, which says, *"The person who sins will die."* We all justify our guilty conscience from wrong behavior with, *"Well, I'm not that bad. I'm really pretty good."* But as Paul says, *"All are under sin. There is none who does good, there is not even one* (Romans 3:9-12)." Compared to a holy God, we're doomed.

If a perfect red balloon represents God's holiness, as the standard for being with Him in Heaven, then how many pins are needed to break it? James 2:10 says, *"For whoever keeps the whole law and yet stumbles in one point, he has become guilty of all."* It's not being good. It's being totally perfect...holy. That's why just being good doesn't cut it. Just one sin breaks God's Law, and our "nobody's perfect" excuse is really a guilty plea.

If you care about your dead soul, read the Book of Romans, and note 11:6, which is the key. *"If it is by grace, it is no longer on the basis of works."* Grace means if you throw a brick through my living room window, I come to your house and wash all of your windows. You get what you don't deserve.

That's grace, and it's not logical. Not to our works-oriented mind.

That's what Jesus did. We all killed our souls with sin, and even one is fatal, and so we deserve punishment for breaking God's Law… death, but instead He died for us. Why?

In Ezekiel 18:23, God reveals His heart, *"Do I have any pleasure in the death of the wicked, rather than that he should turn from his ways and live?"* Again in verse 32, *"For I have no pleasure in the death of anyone who dies (in their sins). Therefore, repent and live."* God loves you, but He can't ignore your guilt. So Jesus lovingly took your place.

Jesus Christ, when just good is not good enough. That's grace (Ephesians 2:1-9).

Week 14:
Gardening with General Patton

"For since by a man came death, by a man also came the resurrection of the dead. For as in Adam all die, so also in Christ all will be made alive (1 Corinthians 15:21-22)."

At our house, Mother's Day is all about death.

My wife loves flowers, which means seeds go into the ground to die with the hope that something new pops up beautiful and alive. It's a good "death" for the seeds and my garden-savvy wife looks forward to caring for some gorgeous flowers.

First Corinthians 15 is the Bible's "gardening chapter." It's also about planting seeds (death), hoping a new life results (resurrection). Do you see your death that way, as a good thing? According to the Bible, death can be a great event, a miraculous change to be anticipated with intense joy, just as we do with our Mother's Day flowers.

Patton knew death, but he didn't fear it and wisely asked, *"Did you ever stop to think that death may be more exciting than life?"* The Apostle Paul agreed and said, *"...to die is gain."* For a genuine believer, death is a friend that brings us eyeball to eyeball with Jesus Christ! That's mighty good news, if you've trusted Christ for your salvation.

But if your sin remains, then you should fear death and the coming judgment (and don't kid yourself and think you're not that bad. If you sin just three times a day and live 70 years, that's over 76,000 sins! A just God cannot be righteous and ignore that.)

Those 76,000 transgressions are a moot point, however, because we're all born with a sin disease that's fatal. Paul said, *"...by a man came death...as in Adam all die."* Bob Dylan agreed and wrote, *"I was blinded by the Devil, born already ruined, stone cold dead as I stepped out of the womb."*

If you're a human being, then you're contaminated by heredity with Adam's sin. Sin is fatal and death is certain (Romans 6:23). There is no escaping it.

Despite that, death can be a friend…if you repent and believe. The litmus test of your belief is your complete assurance when death arrives, as Paul wrote:

But we do not want you to be uninformed, brethren, about those who are asleep, so that you will not grieve as do the rest who have no hope. For if we believe that Jesus died and rose again, even so God will bring with Him those who have fallen asleep in Jesus. For this we say to you by the word of the Lord, that we who are alive and remain until the coming of the Lord, will not precede those who have fallen asleep. For the Lord Himself will descend from heaven with a shout, with the voice of the archangel and with the trumpet of God, and the dead in Christ will rise first. Then we who are alive and remain will be caught up together with them in the clouds to meet the Lord in the air, and so we shall always be with the Lord. Therefore comfort one another with these words.

There are two types of people facing death, those who grieve with hope and those who grieve without it. For a genuine Christian, it's not a loss at all. It's a tremendous gain to pop up again beautiful and alive with Christ.

Week 15:
Why the Bible Doesn't Suck

"All Scripture is inspired by God...(2 Timothy 3:16)."

My mom always told me to read the Bible, the number one bestseller of all-time.

It had great stuff in it she promised…wars, sex, murder, giants, miracles, angels, and demons. But is it reliable as God's Word to speak to us today? Let's look at just the New Testament, and the two primary questions that guide linguistic scholar's textual criticisms:

• How many copies are there to examine and compare?

• How close in time are the oldest copies to the originals?

The more copies that exist, and the closer in time the copies are to the original, the more accurate the results. Ancient works like Josephus or Thucydides are rarely questioned as being authentic in authorship or content, but Josephus has only nine copies and Thucydides has just eight copies.

All the other major works of note from ancient history such as Plato (7), Caesar (10), Pliny (7), Euripides (9), Tacitus (20), and Herodotus (8) are 20 copies or less, and usually much less! Only Sophocles (193) and Aristotle (49) have more than 20.

The New Testament has almost 25,000 copies!

The next closest document would be Homer's *Iliad* with 643 copies with a 500-year gap. Ironically, none of these other manuscripts are contested, despite an 800 – 2,000 year gap from the originals to the copies.

Conversely, one piece of John's gospel is dated to within 25 years after the original was written!

Sir Frederic Kenyon, former director of the British Museum, said, *"In no other case is the interval of time between the composition of the book and the date of the earliest manuscripts so short as in that of the New Testament. The last foundation for any doubt that the Scriptures have come down to us substantially as they were written has now been removed."*

More importantly, these New Testament copies have a 99.5% accuracy rate!

New Testament specialist Daniel Wallace says there are about 300,000 individual variations of the text of the New Testament, but that this number is very misleading. Most of the differences are inconsequential--spelling errors, inverted phrases and the like. A side-by-side comparison between the two main text families (the Majority Text and the Modern Critical Text) shows agreement at a full 98% of the time.

Of the remaining differences, virtually all yield to vigorous textual criticism. This means that our New Testament is 99.5% textually pure. In the entire text of 20,000 lines, only 40 lines are in doubt (about 400 words), and none affects any significant doctrine!

Greek scholar D.A. Carson sums it up this way: *"The purity of text is of such a substantial nature that nothing we believe to be true, and nothing we are commanded to do, is in any way jeopardized by the variants."*

So if God authored the Bible, and He meant it to be His primary communication device to us, do you think He would, as the all-powerful Creator of life, supernaturally protect its contents…to communicate a message to you?

Week 16:
Why the Bible Doesn't Suck II

"All Scripture is inspired by God...(2 Timothy 3:16)."

Last time we discussed the credibility of the New Testament. Now we'll consider the Old Testament's viability as God's primary communication to us.

In 1947, a Bedouin teenager crawled into a cave in Qumran, Israel and found some clay jars that he hoped were filled with treasure. What he found was just some old scrolls, but they turned out to be more valuable than treasure and launched an 11-year search that produced almost 900 manuscripts.

It was the largest biblical manuscript discovery of all time! They ranged from full scrolls (almost 28 feet long) to fragments written in Hebrew, Greek, and Aramaic on papyrus, parchment, and bronze. Every one of the 66 Old Testament books was represented, except the Book of Esther.

The scrolls were also the oldest manuscripts ever found! Before this find, the oldest was dated to 1008 A.D. The oldest Qumran scroll is from about 250 B.C. and the latest to 68 A.D., which is exciting because the closer to the time of the manuscript's origins and the actual event recorded, the more reliable the text (a huge corroborating factor in ancient textual criticism). This was more than a 1,000-year leap!

Together, as the largest and oldest find, these scrolls were pure archaeological gold because when compared with current manuscripts, they confirmed the reliability of the Old Testament in dramatic similarity. To fully appreciate this find, and its precision in content, we need to understand the two primary questions for linguistic scholars:

• How many copies are there to examine and compare?

- How close in time are the oldest copies to the originals?

So the more copies that exist and the closer in time they are to the original, the more accurate the results. Consider these famously accepted and reliable ancient works:

Josephus has nine copies (400 years later) and Thucydides has eight copies (1,300 years later). Plato (7), Caesar (10), Pliny (7), Euripides (9), Tacitus (20), and Herodotus (8) are 20 copies or less. Only Homer's *Iliad* (643), Sophocles (193), and Aristotle (49) have more than 20 copies.

The Old Testament has over 10,000 copies and the Qumran scrolls now move the date to only 150 years after the event–Malachi in 400 B.C. In literary circles, this is not only unheard of, but pure gold for reliability! Unbelievably, there's even more supernatural evidence in the content of these 10,000 copies.

When comparing the Dead Sea Scrolls and the oldest previous texts from 1008 A.D., it is basically a perfect match! This incredible detail over centuries proves that the copying methods used by the scribes were very sophisticated and successful.

They had numerical systems to ensure each page was exact. They counted the number of lines, letters, and words per page of the new copy and then checked them with the original. If they didn't match perfectly, they destroyed the copy.

So why did God supernaturally author and protect the Bible? Perhaps He has something important to say to you…personally. Maybe cracking open a Bible and reading some of it, say the Gospel of John or Luke, is a good idea. I'll wager you'll find more than Bedouin treasure.

Week 17: Empty

"If righteousness comes through the Law, then Christ died needlessly (Galatians 2:21)."

I was afraid to pull the trigger, and with good reason.

Older than dirt, this gifted shotgun looked like it had not been fired in 60 years, so I bravely did what any real guy would do…I took it to a gunsmith.

After a few months, he said it was fixed and safe to fire. Today, it's still empty. I have not pulled the trigger…yet.

For me, it's a matter of trust that this guy (who I don't know) says it's safe, but is it, really? Popping a 20-gauge shell in the chamber, putting it up to my cheek, and pulling the trigger is a big step of faith on just his say-so. Unlike a plastic surgeon, talk is cheap.

If I really believe, I'll act on his promise. Believing is that simple, and that hard.

And so it is with Jesus. Faith to take Him at His word, believing that His death on the cross pays for your sins, and that His tomb is empty is easy…to say. But is just "saying" real saving, eternal faith, or is it just an intellectual assent (like believing in Napoleon or Lincoln)? How can you be sure your faith is genuine and not just acknowledging a fact?

The Apostle James, and half-brother of Jesus, said, *"faith without works is dead."* If you really believe, there will be a transformation because the Holy Spirit enters your body, and good works will flow from your faith. God uses outward and visible faith proofs of this inward and invisible change to tell the world, you "pulled the trigger." What proofs?

In the Old Testament, circumcision was a faith proof, but Israel could not even keep the Ten Commandments, let alone the extensive

Jewish Law. The Law was really a spiritual thermometer to show how sin-sick we all are, that being right with God isn't about doing good works. Besides, if it made lawbreakers right and holy, why did Jesus have to die?

Do you know how to never break the Law? The only way is to have no Law to break. So that's what Jesus did. Jesus was the only one to keep the Law with a sinless life, and as a perfect man, and God, His sacrifice freed us from trying (to be good, keeping the Law), to instead just believing in His work. But again, what is genuine pulling the trigger faith?

Action. In the New Testament, baptism was faith proof of your unseen belief, but getting wet doesn't save you anymore than circumcision made an Israelite a believer. God has always operated on faith and grace; beginning with Abraham's faith, long before the Law was given to Moses (Romans 4). Again, what else constitutes saving faith? Repentance.

James says, *"Even the demons believe."* If they believe in Jesus, and they aren't going to Heaven, what's the difference in your faith and theirs? The answer is…surrendering your will (repent means to change your mind). So stop trying to be good (you can't keep the 10 Commandments either). Ask Him to forgive you, once and for all, based on His work.

Now, I've changed my mind, and by faith…I'm going to go fire my gun. Happy Easter!

Week 18: Earn it!

"If righteousness comes through the Law, then Christ died needlessly (Galatians 2:21)."

Chances are you've never heard of Frederick "Fritz" Niland, but you've seen the famous movie that his life inspired, "Saving Private Ryan."

Sgt. Niland was sent home after the reported deaths of his three brothers (Edward shot down over Burma, Robert killed on D-Day, and Preston killed June 7th near Utah Beach).

In the film, Captain Miller searches for Private Ryan to send him home and like Mrs. Niland, spare Ryan's mother from losing all four sons. After finding Ryan, and losing all of his men, a wounded Miller, seconds from eternity says, *"Earn this."* Then he draws Ryan closer and whispers, *"Earn it!"*

This scene then morphs Ryan into an old man at Normandy Cemetery.

A tearful Ryan, aware of their sacrifice for him asks his wife, *"Tell me I have led a good life. Tell me I'm a good man."* She reassures him, and then he stands back, and salutes Miller's grave as the camera focuses on his white cross.

That cross and Miller's last words always struck me as ironic because we cannot "earn" the salvation the cross represents by "being a good man." The whole point of the cross demonstrates how helpless we are as violators of God's Law (Isaiah 59:2). We can't earn a right standing by our leper-like efforts to bridge the holy gap (Isaiah 64:6).

Yet, most of us think we are good, or at least good enough.

The Bible teaches just the opposite; we fall short. *"For all have sinned and fall short of the glory of God* (Romans 3:23)."* It's not being good, it's being perfect. *"You are to be perfect as your Heavenly Father is perfect* (Matthew 5:48)." Any honest person knows they're not good enough compared to His absolute perfection. Sound like an unfair standard?

Consider two questions.

If you can get to Heaven by being good, *"If righteousness comes through* (keeping) *the Law,"* then why did Jesus die? If your "good life" is enough, then Jesus died for nothing.

Secondly, even if you're a "good man" like Ryan, have you ever broken one of the Ten Commandments? The Bible is clear that one sin makes you guilty of every sin. *"For whoever keeps the whole law and yet stumbles in one point, he has become guilty of all* (James 2:10)."

God doesn't weigh good and bad deeds. His standard is perfection, and nobody's perfect. Having to be perfect is not good news, but it makes sense if you want to be with a sinless God in a sinless Heaven.

The good news is you can become as righteous as God Himself and meet His standard of perfection through Jesus' sacrifice on the cross. *"He made Him* (Jesus) *who knew no sin to be sin on our behalf, so that we might become the righteousness of God in Him* (2 Corinthians 5:21)." God sees you *"in Him"* through the Jesus filter.

His sacrifice (Miller) saved you (Ryan), and like Ryan, you did nothing to earn it. That's grace, unearned favor.

Week 19:
I Triple-Dog-Dare Ya'!

"...and while hearing, they may see and not perceive, and while hearing, they may hear and not understand, otherwise they might return and be forgiven (Mark 4:1-12)."

A Christmas classic in our home has a pole-licking scene from a schoolyard dare. Here's my dare to you. Let's see if it sticks.

"He began to teach again by the sea. And such a very large crowd gathered to Him that He got into a boat in the sea and sat down; and the whole crowd was by the sea on the land. And He was teaching them many things in parables, and was saying to them in His teaching, 'Listen to this! Behold, the sower went out to sow; as he was sowing, some seed fell beside the road, and the birds came and ate it up. Other seed fell on the rocky ground where it did not have much soil; and immediately it sprang up because it had no depth of soil. And after the sun had risen, it was scorched; and because it had no root, it withered away. Other seed fell among the thorns, and the thorns came up and choked it, and it yielded no crop. Other seeds fell into the good soil, and as they grew up and increased, they yielded a crop and produced thirty, sixty, and a hundredfold.'"

And He was saying, "He who has ears to hear, let him hear."

*As soon as He was alone, His followers, along with the twelve, began asking Him about the parables. And He was saying to them, "To you has been given <u>the mystery of the kingdom of God</u>, but those who are outside get everything in parables, so that while seeing, **they may see and not perceive, and while hearing, they may hear and not understand, otherwise they might return and be forgiven** (Mark 4:1-12)."*

If I told you that 90% of American homes have indoor plumbing, but only 11% use it, would you think that odd?

According to *LifeWay Research*, 90% of Americans own a Bible, but only 11% have read the entire book. When I've asked people how much of it they've seriously read (and I've asked thousands) most admit less than 10%. Why is that?

Consider Jesus' explanation, *"The sower sows the word. These are the ones who are beside the road where the word is sown; and when they hear, immediately Satan comes and takes away the word which has been sown in them."* According to Jesus, Satan is real and actively prevents you from hearing and understanding the Bible because he doesn't want you to know God's big mystery.

Rather than give away Jesus' big secret, let's test His spiritual battle claim with a dare (Ephesians 6:12). Try to read the Gospel of John straight through (it'll take two hours). No matter how hard you try, it will be nearly impossible. Give it a shot and wait to see the excuses and obstacles that just pop up.

That's Satan doing his job.

Or maybe try reading just two small chapters with similar parables (Matthew 13, Luke 8), but I bet he'll prevent you from reading these too. Hopefully I'm wrong and you finish John's Gospel because then you'll know Jesus' big secret…if you have ears to hear.

Week 20:
My Brother Died Today

"For we know that if the earthly tent which is our house is torn down, we have a building from God, a house not made with hands, eternal in the heavens. For indeed in this house we groan, longing to be clothed with our dwelling from heaven, inasmuch as we, having put it on, will not be found naked. For indeed while we are in this tent, we groan, being burdened, because we do not want to be unclothed but to be clothed, so that what is mortal will be swallowed up by life. Now He who prepared us for this very purpose is God, who gave to us the Spirit as a pledge (2 Corinthians 5:1-5)."

Fred was 63.

Pancreatic cancer took a visible toll and took him fast. As sad as the last two weeks have been, today is also pretty exciting because Fred surrendered to Jesus Christ many years ago.

Today, right now, Fred is with the *"firstborn from the dead,"* eyeball to eyeball with Jesus of Nazareth. Wow! That's mind-blowing!

I'm very sad and miss him, but if the resurrection is true (and I've bet my life on it as a fact) then this is also a celebration! Weird, I know, but either Jesus did rise from the dead and we have a whole new world to enjoy with Him forever with our redeemed loved ones, or as Paul said, *"we are of all men most to be pitied."*

When death comes, religious mumbo jumbo is the most worthless and empty thing imaginable, trying to be good with man-made traditions. Death silences all tripe.

That's religion, but I'm talking about an empty tomb in Jerusalem. This is not "Religious Thoughts" as the column is named. This column should be called "Death is Dead Thoughts" or "Jesus is Alive Thoughts." It's about the man Who came back to life, God-in-the-flesh, rescuing us!

Watching the visible cancer slowly destroy Fred's mortal tent reminded me of the invisible cancer we all share (sin). We are all dead spiritually because of sin, and in the process of dying physically too (Ephesians 2:1). A hereditary "cancer" passed down from Adam. Paul said in Romans, *"For as in Adam all die, so also in Christ all will be made alive."*

Thankfully, Jesus proved that His death satisfied God's requirement to solve the sin and death problem when He rose from the dead and killed death. If you are *"in Christ"* then your grave can be just as empty. How can you be sure and excited about your death, absolutely, 100 percent sure death has no sting for you? The answer is above, in 2 Corinthians 5:5.

God offers a "down payment" to guarantee He will follow through on His commitment to save you from your spiritual cancer. His pledge––a thing that is given as security for the fulfillment of a contract or the payment of a debt––or "earnest money" as we say in a business transaction, is the Holy Spirit Himself.

His deal to you is this…give up. Surrender. Stop trying to be good enough.

A corpse can't do anything, and spiritually you are a corpse. Let Him take charge of you, body and soul, and invite His Spirit into your body to be in command. It's simple. Repent and believe.

Paul summed it up in 1 Corinthians 6:19-20, *"Or do you not know that your body is a temple of the Holy Spirit who is in you, whom you have from God, and that you are not your own? For you have been bought with a price: therefore glorify God in your body."*

You can be absolutely certain your death is dead too, if the Holy Spirit is inside of your body because you asked Him to come in on His terms…total surrender *("not your own")*. You are not a Christian if He is not inside of you right now.

Fred didn't live a perfect life, but he had the Pledge inside of his earthly tent. God guarantees this transaction with a down payment of Himself. An empty grave in Jerusalem is darn good collateral that God will complete His deal with you. Without Him, you are spiritually naked and in grave danger (Jeremiah 17:13).

Week 21: Dust Two Dust

"The scribes and the Pharisees brought a woman caught in adultery, and having set her in the center of the court, they said to Him, "Teacher, this woman has been caught in adultery, in the very act. "Now in the Law Moses commanded us to stone such women; what then do You say?" They were saying this, testing Him, so that they might have grounds for accusing Him. But Jesus stooped down and with His finger wrote on the ground. But when they persisted in asking Him, He straightened up, and said to them, "He who is without sin among you, let him be the first to throw a stone at her." Again He stooped down and wrote on the ground. When they heard it, they began to go out one by one, beginning with the older ones, and He was left alone, and the woman, where she was, in the center of the court. Straightening up, Jesus said to her, "Woman, where are they? Did no one condemn you?" She said, "No one, Lord." And Jesus said, "I do not condemn you, either. Go. From now on sin no more." - John 8

Ever wonder what Jesus wrote in the dust (twice)? Perhaps it was Gomer. Maybe.

In Hosea, the prophet is told to marry an adulteress named Gomer to illustrate the infidelity of Israel to God, her spiritual husband. A Gomer stood before Jesus now, as guilty of violating God's Law as Israel was in Hosea's marriage imagery.

Ironically, all of her accusers were Gomers too! They were an entire nation of Gomers. So maybe writing Gomer was a reminder for whom He came to ransom, just like this sinful woman he forgave?

Perhaps He wrote Jeremiah 17:13 next. It was read during *Yom Kippur* ("ransom of a life" in Hebrew), the holiest day of the year. The Hebrew translation says:

*"Oh YHWH, the Immerser (baptizer) of Israel, all those who leave your way shall be put to shame (embarrassed publicly), those who turn aside from my ways will **have their names written in the dust and blotted out**, for they have departed from YHWH, the fountain of Mayim Hayim (the waters of life)."*

During Yom Kippur, the High Priest bathed in the *Mikveh* bath symbolizing the One who would come as "the" *Mikveh* bath for Israel to wash away her sins permanently. Then, once a year, he entered the Holy of Holies and sprinkled the blood of the sacrificed goat on the Ark of the Covenant's Mercy Seat.

Finally, he placed his hands on another goat, a scapegoat, transferring Israel's sins from him onto it before banishment to die in the wilderness (Leviticus 16). Every year it reminded Gomer that she needed to be ransomed, but it's no longer necessary now (Hebrews 10). Why?

Because in Hebrew Gomer means, "finished," as the final High Priest said on the cross, *"It is finished* (John 19:30)."* He died as the final ransom *"that takes away the sins of the world."* Sinful Gomer cost Him everything, but don't judge prostitute Israel too harshly like the woman's accusers. There are two Gomers in the dust…all the rest of us.

Week 22:
Thus it is Written...Kill Jesus

"From that time Jesus began to show His disciples that He must go to Jerusalem, and suffer many things from the elders and chief priests and scribes, and be killed, and be raised up on the third day (Matthew 16:21)."

According to the Old Testament, the Jewish Messiah must die.

Say what?

It's crazy to think that this is in the Bible, but the ancient prophets were clear that Messiah must be killed...centuries before Jesus was even born!

There are at least four specific references in the Old Testament that the Messiah would be killed. Psalm 22 was written around 967 BC, Isaiah 53 about 740 BC, Zechariah 12:10 around 520 BC, and Daniel 9:26 in 164 BC.

For the Jews, this is a serious conundrum. Their hope, the Messiah, must be cut off and die. So how then can He be a triumphant King like David and save Israel?

I was discussing this problem and Jesus as the answer with a Jewish man. His problem with a Jewish carpenter's claim to be God was that all men are sinners, and therefore a man from Nazareth could not possibly be God. Pretty simple logic...at first glance.

"So the Almighty made everything, but can't reveal Himself to us in any form He chooses...even as a man?" I asked. He nodded, *"All men are sinners. Therefore, men cannot be God."*

"But according to your Scriptures Messiah must die. God's power isn't limited by what we think He should do," I offered. *"He could appear as a talking kumquat if He wanted to, but if relating to us as humans is paramount, it seems logical He'd become a man and*

thus make this prophesied death possible. After all, if He wanted to save ants, He'd have become an ant."

His objection was sound–all sinners die because of sin (Ezekiel 18:20). This spiritual disease infects us all (Romans 6:23), and since God is holy and eternal then He cannot die, as humans must, right? So how then can Messiah (God) die as it is written centuries beforehand?

It's possible because He can choose to die…not because "of" sin like our curse requires, but "for" sin to rescue us. The Old Testament is clear that the Messiah must die, and that can happen only if He's human, and therefore He must remain sinless until He dies, just as it is written (Luke 24:46). So why does this matter?

Because these four predictions came centuries before Jesus was born!

He even told His disciples before He gave up His life…and that He'd rise again. This predicted "before event" gives us confidence in the truth of the "after event." Jesus proved He is the God-Man, God-in-the-flesh, by being raised from the dead. Therefore, He has power over sin and death…your death, and your sin. Death is coming for us all. Jesus reversed the curse and made death a welcomed event. If you'll genuinely surrender and trust Him, your grave will be as empty as His.

Week 23:
August 6, 1988

"And again Jesus spoke to them in parables, saying, 'The kingdom of heaven may be compared to a king who gave a wedding feast for his son, and sent his servants to call those who were invited to the wedding feast, but they would not come (Matthew 22:1-3).'"

Almost 30 years ago, I sent Bob Dylan an invitation to our wedding, and just like the guests in this parable, my hero didn't come. I admit, it was a long-shot.

Despite that "snub," inspired by a Dylan song called, *"The Groom's Still Waiting At The Altar,"* I wrote this for the back of our wedding program for those who did come:

Well, it's hard to believe that our wedding day is finally here! We've been looking forward to this day (and sharing it with all of you) for a long time. Excitement, anticipation, and joy are just a few of the emotions that we've been experiencing in thinking about our wedding day. The day that I am finally united with my bride, and she with me! But even more important than our wedding day is another wedding day that we'd like to invite all of you to now.

This wedding is a very special one because it is a wedding that is being arranged by God and everyone is invited. It says in the Bible that Jesus Christ is the groom and that the bride will be everyone who accepts His proposal. This very unique couple will one day be united forever in Heaven, but only those people who choose to respond can be His bride. When I asked Amy to marry me, it was then up to her to decide whether or not she wanted to choose to enter into that commitment with me. It wasn't until she did accept my proposal that we could get to the point we are at here today.

In the exact same way, each of you must consider Jesus' proposal. "Proposal?" you may be wondering. "When did Jesus ever propose to me?" Well, He said it a long time ago, but more important than what He said is what He did. Jesus demonstrated His own love toward us, in that while we were sinners, Christ died for us. That was His proposal, one of action. In the same way, through our action, we must respond to that sacrifice by accepting Him as our groom.

Several years ago, Amy and I both decided to accept His proposal of love. Since then, we have both been anxiously awaiting the day that we are united with Him as our groom. As you watch our ceremony today, we'd like you to think of the wedding that is yet to be in Heaven. We'd like to see all of you there too, but that is your own personal decision. After all, that's precisely what love is, a personal choice.

Thanks for sharing this wedding with us. Hope to see you at the other one too.

So the next time you go to a wedding, think about His proposal to you, but realize He won't wait forever. Eventually, there will be a wedding with or without you, just as ours was…even without Bob Dylan (Revelation 19:7).

Week 24: God's Odds

"Declaring the end from the beginning, and from ancient times things which have not been done...(Isaiah 46:10)."

Did you know that you have a better chance to become President than winning the lottery (10 million to one)? It's true, but what are the odds of predicting the future? A million to one maybe?

God says He sees the end before the beginning…every time! Let's look at one of His prophecies from 590 B.C. about the city of Tyre in Ezekiel chapter 26.

"Therefore thus says the Lord God, 'Behold, I am against you, O Tyre, and I will bring up many nations against you, as the sea brings up its waves. 'They will destroy the walls of Tyre and break down her towers; and I will scrape her debris from her and make her a bare rock. 'She will be a place for the spreading of nets in the midst of the sea, for I have spoken,' declares the Lord God, 'and she will become spoil for the nations."

"For thus says the Lord God, "Behold, I will bring upon Tyre from the north Nebuchadnezzar king of Babylon, king of kings, with horses, chariots, cavalry and a great army."

"Also they will make a spoil of your riches and a prey of your merchandise, break down your walls and destroy your pleasant houses, and throw your stones and your timbers and your debris into the water."

"I will make you a bare rock; you will be a place for the spreading of nets. You will be built no more, for I the Lord have spoken," declares the Lord God."

"Then all the princes of the sea will go down from their thrones, remove their robes and strip off their embroidered garments. They will clothe themselves with trembling; they will sit on the ground, tremble every moment and be appalled at you."

Ezekiel prophesies Tyre's destruction with these specifics:

1. Nebuchadnezzar will conquer Tyre.

2. Other nations will take part in its destruction.

3. Tyre will be flat like the top of a rock.

4. Tyre will become a place to spread nets.

5. Tyre's stones and timber will be laid in the sea.

6. Other cities will fear because of Tyre's destruction.

7. Tyre won't be rebuilt.

It all came to pass when Nebuchadnezzar laid siege in 586 B.C., and then Alexander the Great finished it off 241 years later. According to Dr Peter W. Stoner in *Science Speaks*, "The odds of this happening are 75 million to one."

My point? Buy a Bible, not a lottery ticket.

Week 25: Drop Dead!

> "And inasmuch as it is appointed for men to die once and after this comes judgment (Hebrews 9:27)."

That's my Easter message to you. No chocolate bunnies or candy eggs.

I mean we're all going to do that some day, so why not use it as a greeting this Easter? Walk into church on Sunday and with a big smile, let'em have it with gusto:

"Drop dead!"

Let me explain. This verse in the Book of Hebrews makes it crystal clear that there is no reincarnation, no purgatory, and no other escape from His righteous judgment.

We will all die, and then a righteous and unerring Judge will judge all of us. Simple theology. His criteria? He Himself is the standard (Matthew 5:48). Absolute perfection. Holiness.

Utter and glaring bright righteousness where not one sin, mistake, or error will be squinted at. Anything less than absolute perfect morality will be judged wanting. Think about it. If God let us sinners into His Heaven it'd be the same mess we have now on earth, right?

Can't have sin in Heaven. Sin has to be eliminated to have holiness.

But on the other hand, nobody's perfect, right? We've all broken a commandment or two. Everyone has stolen something or lied or dishonored parents. So how is this fair if we all fall short of His perfect standard? Seems rigged. Shouldn't He weigh our good deeds against our bad deeds? Nope. That's not perfect and absolute 100 % holiness.

As James said, *"For whoever keeps the whole law and yet stumbles in one point, he has become guilty of all (James 2:10)."*

That's the bad news. According to James, we are all guilty of breaking all the commandments because just one sin kills perfection. Now here's the good news that makes Easter the greatest holiday of all time…we don't have to stay dead as Jesus proved when He left His grave EMPTY!

That's our guarantee that death and punishment can be taken care of, a substitute takes all of our righteous judgment for sin for us, as Peter said, *"For Christ also died for sins once for all, the just for the unjust, so that He might bring us to God, having been put to death in the flesh, but made alive in the spirit (1 Peter 3:18)."*

The only catch is in Mark 1:14-15, *"Repent and believe."*

Repent is a fancy word for changing your mind. Instead of going left, you go right. Instead of ham, you chose liver for Easter dinner. Also known as surrendering, admitting you're defeated and lost. Instead of doing what you want, you surrender to what He wants… all of it.

And believing isn't in your head. It's in your heart. It means action. You do it because you believe it. You take a stand, like getting baptized; something He wants and your first proof of believing (Matthew 29:18-20). Symbolically you "drop dead" into the water, and come up out of "death" like Jesus Christ…a new and forgiven person by faith in His death and resurrection…with your own empty grave in the water.

So have a Happy Easter, have some liver for dinner, and drop dead…please!

Week 26: Mother Nature

"For since the creation of the world His invisible attributes, His eternal power and divine nature, have been clearly seen, being understood through what has been made, so that they are without excuse. For even though they knew God, they did not honor Him as God or give thanks, but they became futile in their speculations, and their foolish heart was darkened (Romans 1:20-21)."

"It's not nice to fool Mother Nature!"

That iconic margarine commercial made a big impact on consumers in the 70's.

If you're too young to remember, it showed Mother Nature tasting what she thought was butter, and then when the narrator tells her she's wrong, she angrily flashes her thunder and lightning threat with this catchy phrase. It had a pretty successful run.

Pretty effective advertising as her saying is still used today, especially when the weather acts up. So why mention this commercial? Frankly, I'm fed up with Mother Nature and cringe every time a weatherman uses it in their forecast.

It's subtle, I know, but it undermines God's place as our Creator. As Paul said in Romans, everyone knows He's real because of the marvel of nature. Before you judge me as a nitpicker imagine this scenario.

You're watching the weather tonight and there's crazy stuff going on, from tornadoes to floods, to hail and ice, and the weatherman says, *"God has really let loose on the Midwest with His power as this severe storm barrels down on Michigan."* It'd never happen, and if it did happen that person would be fired. Doesn't that strike you as odd?

I've never heard a meteorologist attribute the power of acute weather to God, but always to Mother Nature (and she doesn't even exist!) She's no more real than the Tooth Fairy, Santa, or the Easter Bunny (and those last two minimize His rightful place too). The point is this.

Unlike Mother Nature, God is very real and even atheists are *"without excuse."* Just look around as spring bursts forth today. *"His invisible attributes, His eternal power and divine nature, have been clearly seen, being understood through what has been made."* And since we are the pinnacle of His creation, it also means that we are accountable to Him as our Maker (Hebrews 9:27).

As our Creator, He has every right to expect something from us. One day, as our Judge, He will look upon us for His holiness, which apart from Jesus' blood to cover our sins and make us holy, just doesn't exist. As James said, *"For whoever keeps the whole law and yet stumbles in one point, he has become guilty of all."*

We are all guilty, and despite our very best efforts, unlike Mother Nature's faulty taste buds, we can't fool God by our good deeds when our sin remains (Isaiah 64:6). He knows real butter from margarine. Thankfully, He has withheld His thunder and lightning judgment that we deserved, and Jesus joyfully took it for us to make us as holy as God Himself (2 Corinthians 5:21). Now that's a truly iconic message!

Week 27: Wreck-ognize Truth

"I am the way and the truth and the life. No one comes to the Father except through Me (John 14:6)."

I love bumper stickers.

My favorite is, *"God, make me the man my dog thinks I am."* As funny as that one is, there's another one that we've all seen that is a joke too, but in a farcical sense. It's the religious symbols that spell out COEXIST.

It's a joke because these religions contradict each other with their own exclusive claims, but only one is corroborated by a resurrected Man; all the others are founded by dead men, who base their way to God on doing good works to appease Him for their sins (Galatians 2:21).

Truth cannot coexist with lies. Jesus absolutely refutes them all.

And they all completely deny that Jesus is God and the only way to Heaven, as He said, so the bumper sticker is not being intellectually honest.

Only Jesus rose from the dead to prove His statement to be *"the truth."* Christianity is based on Jesus being God and the only way to Heaven, which is either arrogant or true. Two plus two equals four, every…single…time.

Truth is always absolute, and it usually has evidence and witnesses (1 Corinthians 15:1-8).

The Apostles saw Jesus live, die, and come back from the dead, and Peter said the same exclusive thing when arrested for this very truth, *"And there is salvation in no one else; for there is no other name under heaven that has been given among men by which we must be saved (Acts 4:12)."*

These eyewitnesses, who died for this truth and could have evaded execution had they said they made it up, claimed Jesus was the only way to Heaven. Some may die for what they think is true, but no one would die for a lie. *"No other name"* eliminates every other religion, no matter how sincere.

Just because Buddha, Confucius, or Mohammed are sincere doesn't make their religion true. Sincerity can be dead wrong if it's not true. Sincerely driving to Florida by heading west is the wrong way. Jesus is absolutely exclusive by making this claim to be *"the way,"* but He is also <u>inclusive</u> by offering salvation to everyone.

Why does His brash claim bother us?

Because we want everyone to be saved from death and hope all religions lead to God. If so, then mathematics is arrogant because two plus two equals four, and so is geography because Florida is due south, and Jesus is a bald-faced liar if He's not *"the life."*

Jesus made every religion false when He said, *"I am the way and the truth and the life. No one comes to the Father except through Me."*

So you can head west to Florida, and sincerely hit your brakes twice (and say it was four) to not rear-end the car in front of you (with the COEXIST bumper sticker), but if your brake line is cut…sincerity won't save you. The truth is you'll wreck your car.

Week 28: Grammar God

"It is finished (John 19:30)."

I have a confession.

Without Donna, I would not have gotten through my Seventh Grade English class. She reluctantly helped me, and many more times I looked over her shoulder to copy her answers. I'm a cheater. Wherever you are, thanks Donna! I'm in your debt.

As a writer, this is a humbling admission. I still don't get nominative or objective personal pronouns. Grammar is not my strength, but those rules do matter. Why? Our home serves as a perfect example of why rules are so important (and debt has a penalty).

On Tuesday, we paid off our mortgage early. It's a great feeling to be debt-free! When I spoke with the woman at the bank she said we'd get a satisfaction letter confirming that "it is finished." I immediately thought of Jesus' last words on the cross. *Tetelestai*.

In Greek, the New Testament's language, *tetelestai* means, "It is finished." But this verb is in the "perfect tense," which means not only is it done in the past, but also that the result is still ongoing. This past action is continuous.

A "past tense" verb is over and done, but the perfect tense continues…like our home is paid off now, and tomorrow too.

But His dying words seem off, maybe even bad grammar. "I am finished" makes more sense, unless…He's paid off a debt too, and that's precisely what Jesus did. In New Testament times, *tetelestai* was used on documents to show that a bill had been paid in full. So what did God-in-the-flesh pay off if He's holy and has no sin?

He paid our debt.

Nobody's perfect (Romans 3:23). We've all sinned, but this sin-debt is lethal; it makes all of us spiritually dead (Ephesians 2:1), separates us from a holy God (Isaiah 59:2), and results in physical death (Ezekiel 18:20).

We don't like death talk, but it's inescapable. My brother died a few weeks ago and it was so very final. The key, however, is not to die with your sin-debt outstanding or the penalty is eternal death (2 Thessalonians 1:8-9).

But is God fair to judge us with His holy standards if nobody's perfect? Yes, a good judge punishes lawbreakers, but a loving judge would be heartbroken. God solved this problem when He said, *"It is finished."* Debt paid in full, in love. Done deal? Not quite.

God's gift will erase your past, present, and future sin-debts, but like a Christmas gift under the tree it can only be opened if you receive it (John 1:12). Since it's a gift you can't earn it (Ephesians 2:4-9). It's free, but knowing it's there is not receiving it. It's not yours until you take it out from under the Christmas tree and open it.

That's the Christmas Rule.

Grammar also functions on rules, and so does God. If you break His Law, He must be righteous and deal with it. Thankfully, He loved us enough to take our penalty Himself (2 Corinthians 5:21). He acted on His love (Romans 5:8). Now you must act too. Just confess, a humble "Donna" admission, and the free gift is yours (Romans 10:9). Awl cheaters ar welcome!

Week 29:
The Koimeterion Hotel

"Behold, I tell you a mystery; we shall not all sleep, but we shall all be changed (1 Corinthians 15:51)."

I love a good mystery. My wife and I are enjoying a British detective show called *"Vera,"* which is in its ninth season and has become wildly popular.

Contrast that popularity with another mystery folks work very hard to ignore…cemeteries.

Have you ever noticed that they are almost always deserted? Pretty strange.

And yet there's something about a whole life crammed into a headstone that fascinates me. I can't help it; I like cemeteries. My favorite is in Key West, Florida. A tombstone there simply reads, *"I told you I was sick."*

The Apostle Paul wrote that we are all sick too (Romans 3:23), infected with a spiritual cancer that has not only deadened our soul (Ephesians 2:1), but also kills our body. Sin is deadly (Romans 6:23).

Paul also said that even if you are born again–the Holy Spirit is literally inside of your body–your physical death is inevitable, but that thankfully it's no longer fatal for a genuine believer. He likened it to sleep, just like an afternoon nap.

Paul chose a good metaphor. Death looks like sleep, but sleep is only a temporary condition.

You will eventually wake up, whereas death is a permanent separation of soul and body. Paul's warning is that sin makes death inescapable, but that it doesn't need to be permanent. The "change" he references above is to the resurrection where real believers are changed into immortals with a new body, but without sin.

So why do we avoid cemeteries?

Perhaps ignoring death lessens our fear of it and the unknown, but the Bible says it's good to go to funerals because they wake us up to this certain rendezvous (Ecclesiastes 7:1-2). Like cemeteries, funerals remind us of our own transience, that we have an irrevocable appointment with God, and the supreme importance of not gambling with death (2 Corinthians 5:10).

Are you gambling? Or are you one hundred percent positive, without a doubt, and absolutely certain that if you died tonight you'd go to Heaven? The Bible was written for this very purpose (1 John 5:13). Heaven isn't guesswork, you can know for sure. Death can be just a nap!

Your fear of death can end today, and then you can join me for a cemetery stroll because they're not only fascinating historical places, but literally restful. In fact, the Greek word Paul uses for cemetery, *koimeterion*, is also translated as hotel, a "rest house for strangers."

So if He is inside of you, then death is more exciting than life, and no mystery at all.

As Paul said, "*But we do not want you to be uninformed, brethren, about those who are asleep, that you may not grieve, as those who have no hope* (1 Thessalonians 4:13)." Although someone giving away the ending for a mystery is annoying, Paul's spoiler-alert means comfort for our ending…an assured funeral hope…and Jesus' empty tomb proves that hope. Death itself is quite literally dead.

Week 30: Kitchen Kisses

"But only a few things are necessary, really only one... (Luke 10:42)."

"I have learned to kiss the wave that throws me against the Rock of Ages."

What did the great preacher Charles Spurgeon mean by this sentence?

Our answer is two miles from Jerusalem, in a small town called Bethany, where Luke, the Gentile doctor, probably the only Gentile author of a New Testament book, records a clue for us.

Jesus stayed in Bethany several times at the home of two sisters, Martha and Mary. Luke records it in his Gospel in chapter 10, and there's a lot to glean, but the point to catch, the paramount lesson, is this...don't be so busy and worried with life that you ignore Jesus.

The older sister, Martha, reproved Mary, who was not helping her with all the kitchen preparations for their important guest... appearing to be lazy for just sitting around *"listening to the Lord's word, seated at His feet."* But Jesus corrected His hostess. *"You are worried and bothered about so many things,"* Jesus told Martha. *"But Mary has chosen the good part"* because she was quietly spending time with Jesus.

Back to Spurgeon, and being dashed against the rocks by the world's problems.

The great preacher meant that worries and busyness could have two results. The first is natural...it's a negative reaction; we get upset, anxious, and frustrated when the storms of life smash into us. Like Martha, we miss the point, not "kissing" their push to Jesus.

Spurgeon commends his own spiritual growth with the second and preferred reaction, a supernatural response that drove him to his knees...talking with Him (in prayer) and listening to His words (reading the Bible). Getting bashed with busyness and worries can be good if it drives you to the Rock of Ages, to worship Jesus Christ…Who is <u>in control</u>.

Whether you know Jesus or don't, He is saying that only a few things are necessary today, really only one…and that is this—be with Him.

You can ready yourself each day for the world's waves with His help, His comforting words, and not rush off unprepared and vulnerable. Your bothers and worries can be positives, loving shoves into His arms. Could it be He allows this in order to get your attention? Flat on your back means you have to look up.

Beware your "kitchen" distraction that keeps you from Him, the "really only one." Is it your job, your family, or your tasks? Identify it, and put it second to a daily time alone with Him, even 30 minutes can alter your view of the worst wave crashes, even death.

Getting sick and dying is a real wave, and it happened to the brother of Martha and Mary. Death-dashed, they sent for Jesus. Four days later, Jesus arrived, and raised Lazarus from the dead (John 11). They were driven to Him for help. A reminder that "really only one" thing is necessary each day, to worship, which in the Greek means, "draw near to kiss." So leave the kitchen, and worship the One, Who controls even the waves (Matthew 8:27).

Week 31: Flip It

"Truly I say to you, today you will be with Me in Paradise (Luke 23:43)."

I saw a show at the *Wharton Center* at Michigan State on Saturday, "The Illusionists."

These five Broadway magicians were absolutely incredible! They took numerous impossible scenarios and magically flipped them into stunning miracles. With absolute precision, they flipped it. And even in the third row I could not tell how they did it.

On the night of October 29th, 1978, my brother Jack got into his white Ford station wagon, doused himself with a gallon of gasoline, and lit a match. He was 28.

On the night that he blew himself up in his car with gasoline, in the parking lot of a bar in Los Angeles, I was 2,265 miles away in Livonia, Michigan asleep.

That night changed lives in my family. Eternity changed too. At just 17 years old, it was the worst experience of my life. Where do you go after something like that? Who do you talk to for solace and some perspective? I went nowhere for about two years.

On the day of April 3rd, 33 AD, God in the flesh was murdered in Jerusalem, probably naked, definitely whipped, beaten, and bloody, in a public execution on a cross. Two thieves died with Him. As you can imagine, like Jack's death, it was nasty.

That night changed lives in Israel.

For those who knew Jesus, as the promised Old Testament Messiah, it was the absolute worst day of all time, ever. And yet God took the very worst, and flipped it to be the very best, ever…because He didn't stay dead. He walked out of His own grave. God took the worst and made it the best. That's no illusion. It's real magic.

His is the only empty grave on Earth. Death died.

Jack always called me by a nickname. As a baby I wouldn't lie still. Always squirming. That name was Flipper, which he shortened to Flip. That moniker would be a self-fulfilling prophecy of sorts because Jesus flipped me. Two years after Jack entered eternity, I heard the gospel message. Spiritually, I was asleep, until then.

"*In Him, you also, after listening to the message of truth, the gospel of your salvation—having also believed, you were sealed in Him with the Holy Spirit of promise, who is given as a pledge of our inheritance, with a view to the redemption of God's own possession, to the praise of His glory* (Ephesians 1:13-14)."

God flipped my despair and made it a stunning miracle. I heard, believed, and the Holy Spirit entered my body. His seal is a down payment, a legal pledge that guarantees God will complete the "purchase" when I die. Like the thief, when Jesus took his worst day and made it his best, He flipped Flip.

Are you despairing? Paul wrote Romans, the sixth book in the New Testament, to explain the gospel. Give it a read, in a current easy-to-read version (NLT), ask Him to wake you up to understand it, and He'll flip your life too. It's no illusion.

Week 32:
Mythed Me By That Much

"Now these (Bereans) were more noble-minded than those in Thessalonica, for they received the Word with great eagerness, examining the Scriptures daily, to see whether these things were so (Acts 17:11)."

Three weeks before the 75th anniversary of the Normandy invasion, I found myself on Omaha Beach in France. This had been at the top of my Bucket List for years.

The flat expanse overwhelms; there's no cover from the Nazi gunfire that slaughtered our troops. Even a poor marksman with eyes closed couldn't miss killing gobs of men in that open terrain. It was beyond humbling.

When we got back in the car, our French tour guide recounted the story of Raymond Hoback's Bible (he and his brother Bedford of A Company, 116th Infantry were both killed on June 6th where we had literally just stood). Another American soldier found his Bible on the beach and thoughtfully mailed it to the family.

"They were the first to go in and they really didn't have a chance, the Germans were mowing them down as they hit the beach," said Lucille Hoback Boggess, their younger sister. *"My mother always treasured that Bible."*

I asked our guide where he went to church. Sadly, he said he never did, and had been raised with no real comprehension of Jesus. Then he added that no one goes to church in France! I was stunned and asked if he ever read the Bible. He'd never opened one, but there were so many interpretations, why bother?

This was a dangerous myth, perhaps even more deadly than the German guns that had killed over 20,000 Americans by August 21, 1944. Why? Because his eternal destiny hung in the balance, and so I asked him the question I now pose to you.

If God wanted to communicate soul-saving truth about sin, death, and how to get to Heaven…would He make His truth complicated or easy to understand? And furthermore, would He supernaturally preserve that communication from all error and misunderstanding to ensure that you grasped His redemption message?

If I were God, and gave up my life to DIE in your place to save you, I'd use all of my power to keep my message simple, secure, and so easy to understand that even if you weren't very smart you'd still get it.

Speaking of getting smart…Don Adams made this comical phrase in our title famous as Maxwell Smart's explanation for escaping death in the TV show "Get Smart." Missing out on death is precisely the point here.

Unfortunately, most people have never read the Bible and will "myth out" on Heaven by "that much"… just two feet, the distance from their head to their heart. Just like the soldier who found Hoback's Bible said, *"I was walking along the beach D-Day plus one. I came upon the Bible and as most any person would do I picked it up."* So, why not get smart, just pick it up, and be a Berean to see if these things are so? The Hoback family treasured it for a very good reason, and now it's yours to discover why they did.

Week 33: Not Sure

"These things I have written to you...that you may know...
(1 John 5:13)."

The first rule in writing a movie is to be clear.

If the audience can't follow your story, then game over. How much more important is clarity in communicating spiritual truth to a world flooded with disinformation? So who can you trust? How about the very first Writer?

God has written a movie called "Being 100% Sure You're Going to Heaven." It's playing in a Bible near you, and He lays out the logline in 1 John, *"These things I have written to you who believe in the name of the Son of God, in order that you may know that you have eternal life."* That's pretty clear, but most people are still not sure.

Most hope they're good enough to go to Heaven because they haven't done anything really bad and guess they're between the 40-75% range, but the Bible says that you can be 100% certain. That's why God wrote "these things." So how can you be 100% sure?

First, realize nobody's perfect. Since God is perfect (holy), we cannot be with Him in Heaven or our sin would wreck it pretty quick. *"But your iniquities have made a separation between you and your God (Isaiah 59:2)."* Pretty clear, broken and alienated.

Second, good works don't work. Would you accept a million bucks from a leper? *"All our most righteous deeds are like a filthy rag to God (Isaiah 64:6)."* And there is no scale to weigh good deeds and bad deeds. *"Whoever keeps the whole Law and yet stumbles in one point, he has become guilty of all (James 2:10)."* If a big, red balloon represents God's Law, how many pins are needed to break it? No matter how hard you try, you cannot make that balloon perfect again.

It's not about being good; it's about perfection.

Third, God's holiness also means our sin must be punished. A sin a day is over 25,000 in 70 years, and if He ignored it, then He'd be a crooked judge. He solved this problem; loving us and punishing us, by taking it on Himself...only a perfect Person could pay our debt, so God became flesh. *"He made Him (Jesus) who knew no sin, to be sin on our behalf, that we might become the righteousness of God in Him* (2 Corinthians 5:21)." His gift makes you holy, but it's on His terms, and "believing" can be a confusing term.

True faith is action, the plot-point most miss in His story (especially the religious who think their good works matter). Believing is not just acknowledging a fact. Demons believe, but they're not going to Heaven (James 2:19), so what's the difference between your belief and their belief? True, saving faith is repentance, surrendering pride and will.

This action, to take His free gift by faith, is enough to pay for all your sin. Doing good works to gain righteousness is pride, and an insult to His sacrifice (Galatians 2:16, 21). Genuine faith is a humble, thankful surrender, and receiving Him makes you as righteous as God because now He sees you through the camera lens of Jesus. But the Holy Spirit will only come into your heart "theater" if you're showing His other film: "Jesus Alone."

Week 34: The Wait is Over!

"I wait for the Lord, my soul does wait, and in His word do I hope. My soul waits for the Lord, more than watchmen for the morning." –King David (Psalm 130)

You've heard it said, "Death and taxes," but I think we can add one more certainty in life…no one likes to wait.

No one…especially at Christmas when gifts flood our living rooms on December 24th.

In the Old Testament this is a very common theme, to "wait for the Lord." Wait for what? Technically it's on His coming through for you because of His love and goodness toward you, but the culmination of that was in His coming to Bethlehem (Matthew 1:23).

As Isaiah prophesied about 700 years before the Star appeared in Israel's tiny town, the wait would finally end on the first Christmas:

"BEHOLD, THE VIRGIN SHALL BE WITH CHILD AND SHALL BEAR A SON, AND THEY SHALL CALL HIS NAME IMMANUEL," *which translated means,* "GOD WITH US."

The One waited for, for thousands of years by the Jewish people, arrived, in the flesh, as a tiny baby boy. Literally God in the flesh! His miracle birth goes back all the way to the very beginning in Genesis with Abraham's promise to an heir (Genesis 12:3),

"…. in you all the nations of the earth will be blessed."

In the line of Abraham's descendents, the Jews, God Himself would appear and save the world by blessing *"all the nations"* with a second chance. Forgiveness of all our sins. God sealed the salvation covenant with Abraham by walking through a cut up sacrificial animal. He literally "cut a deal" with Abraham (and us) based on death and blood (Genesis 15).

Most objections to Jesus being the promised Messiah, Immanuel (God with us), as a human being cite biblical logic…all men are sinners and therefore the man Jesus could not be God; a logical objection that we experience daily since we have all sinned (Roman 3:23).

But in the objection is an objection to itself.

If all men are sinners (agreed we have all failed God's standard), then we are prone to error, mistakes, and wrong reasoning. Namely, if God wants to appear to us as a mouse or a banana or a donkey… He has the right and power to do so.

Coming to us as a human being would seem to be the most logical way to communicate His ways and desires for us as one Himself. If He wanted to communicate with gerbils, He'd come as a gerbil, right?

And furthermore, if He came to break the death sentence of Sin, to end the blessing wait for *"all the nations,"* it would be a perfect form to meet the requirements of the Passover sacrifice as a perfect lamb to be killed, providing He did live a perfect life.

The Christmas deal that God cut with His own blood, from Abraham to Bethlehem to the cross means the wait is over, but like all Christmas gifts you have to receive it.

"But as many as received Him, to them He gave the right to become children of God, even to those who believe in His name (John 1:12)."

Week 35:
When the Deal Goes Down

"Jesus...abolished Death and brought Life and Immortality to light (2 Timothy 1:10)."

A good friend lies in the ICU right now, and will most likely be dead before this column goes to press. It breaks my heart.

Eternity looms for Jeff, as it did for Paul when he wrote these words, his last letter to Timothy before Rome chopped off his head. Immortality finally revealed.

> Each invisible prayer is like a cloud in the air, Tomorrow keeps turning around
> We live and we die, we know not why, But I'll be with you when the deal goes down

Fortunately, Jeff's a Christian (and a fellow Bob Dylan fan). We went to see Dylan at the *Wharton Center* last year (our third time seeing him together since Bob became a Christian) and Jeff wondered if this was the last time we'd see Bob (since Dylan is 79).

> The midnight rain follows the train, We all wear the same thorny crown
> Soul to soul, our shadows roll, And I'll be with you when the deal goes down

Bob has a song, "When the Deal Goes Down" that talks about not being alone in Death for the Christian.

Jeff is living these lyrics right now. What an immense comfort to his wife who sits by his side tonight, praying, knowing their separation is only momentary. And, that Jesus will usher him into eternity to be safe from any harm. Death abolished.

> More frailer than the flowers, these precious hours, That keep us so tightly bound

> You come to my eyes like a vision from the skies, And I'll be with you when the deal goes down

Warren Weirsbe once said, *"If you're born once, you die twice; born twice and you die only once."* In other words, Death cannot hold you in the grave if you're born again by the Spirit. But if you ignore Jesus, the one who conquered Death, and are only born physically, then a Second Death awaits you to pay for your own sin. It's your choice.

> In this earthly domain, full of disappointment and pain, You'll never see me frown
> I owe my heart to you, and that's sayin' it true, And I'll be with you when the deal goes down

Those are some excerpts from Dylan's classic song, and now I'll take a shot at a verse:

> The rich and the poor, they always want more, Immortality too far from shore. They cut and they duck, but Death still runs amok, and stands alone at their door.

> Asleep at the switch, there's always some itch, thinking there's bound to be more. But the road always ends, with no payment for sins, they're left alone, when the deal goes down.

Maybe I'm not Dylan, but we both know without Jesus you haven't got a chance in your ICU.

If Jesus rose from the dead, and revealed Life and Immortality, can you give me one good reason why you wouldn't bend your knee tonight and repent? I can see Jeff, a man "Forever Young," offering a thumbs-up right now on that ICU bed. Choose Life.

Week 36: Gomer or Goner?

"But Jesus stooped down, and with His finger wrote on the ground (John 8:1-11)."

Did you know that General Washington made Thanksgiving an official holiday in 1777, long before Lincoln made it our national holiday in 1863? Most don't know that tidbit.

Both men wanted to thank God for His blessings on America since 1620, but what about you? What are you the most thankful for on this Thanksgiving?

For me, it's doing nothing. Let me explain.

With a Catholic father and an Episcopal mother I had a good religious foundation, but I thought forgiveness depended on my efforts. If I did more good things than bad things, then God would let me into Heaven, kind of like a cosmic scale weighing out my life choices.

I was wrong. Doing something for God to balance out my sins was delusional. Imagine a contagious leper offering you a gift. Two examples show that we can do nothing to earn God's favor.

Remember what Jesus said to the thief crucified with Him in Luke 23? *"Today you will be with Me in Paradise."* What good works could he do in those final minutes to outweigh a lifetime of sins?

And the adulterous woman in John 8 when Jesus said to her, *"Neither do I condemn you."* What good works could she do in those few minutes to outweigh a lifetime of sins?

When you compare your works against His holiness, then we're all goners, as Isaiah 64:6 says, *"...all our righteous deeds are like a filthy garment* (which in Hebrew is likened to a menstrual cloth).*"* Our best is worthless.

So what did Jesus write in the dirt?

Perhaps it was the name of the prophet Hosea's wife. She was a harlot too, but God told Hosea to marry her, symbolically depicting Israel's unfaithfulness to God. Later on, she was redeemed and brought back to her husband. Her name was Gomer, which means, *"complete"* in Hebrew, and Jesus' last words on the cross, *"It is finished* (or complete)."

Admitting that my sin separates me from God is the first step, guilty as charged (Isaiah 59:2), and that my salvation depends on what He completed on the cross—only His bloody sacrifice cancelled my debt (Colossians 2:13-14). Nothing else. My cosmic scale is demolished.

Like the adulterous woman and the dying thief, we're all criminals, but as Ephesians 2:8-9 says, doing nothing is the key, *"...by grace you have been saved through faith; and that not of yourselves, it is the gift of God; not as a result of works that no one should boast."* You don't work for a gift; you just receive it (John 1:12).

This takes humility to do nothing, to admit guilt, and simply surrender, but that's what a Gomer is…a desperate harlot or a convicted thief, helpless, only complete by His work on the cross (Galatians 2:16-21).

So on this Thanksgiving I'm most thankful for being a Gomer, one brought back to her husband who could do nothing to be redeemed from my harlotry, but no longer a Goner.

Week 37: What Does Satan Believe About Our Election?

"It's better to go to funerals, than parties because Death is the end of every man and the living take it to heart."
–King Solomon

On January 5, 1962, one of my favorite *Twilight Zone* episodes aired when I was not even a year old. Rodman Serling's raspy introduction to it is still a classic all these years later.

"An old woman living in a nightmare, an old woman who has fought a thousand battles with death and always won," croaked the familiar voice. *"Now she's faced with a grim decision—whether or not to open a door. And in some strange and frightening way she knows that this seemingly ordinary door leads to…**The Twilight Zone**."*

"Nothing in the Dark" told the story of an old woman who would not open her door for fear it would be Death, and if Death touched her she would die (Ironically, Death was played by Robert Redford, who is now 80 years old, and the role is quite reversed).

What does this have to do with Satan and our polarizing presidential election in a few weeks? Everything. Like the magician's ploy, it's all misdirection so we don't see the real trick. Pretending to be a wounded policeman, Redford fooled her into opening the door.

Clive Staples Lewis wrote *The Screwtape Letters* in 1942 as a series of letters from an old, retired demon named Screwtape to his nephew, Wormwood, a neophyte demon still learning his job…how to distract us from our real issue of sin and death and judgment.

Here's a sample of their scheme to keep us from our real problem, as sick patients:

My Dear Wormwood,

Be sure that the patient remains completely fixated on politics. Arguments, political gossip, and obsessing on the faults of people they have never met serves as an excellent distraction from advancing in personal virtue, character, and the things the patient can control.

Make sure to keep the patient in a constant state of angst, frustration, and general disdain towards the rest of the human race in order to avoid any kind of charity or inner peace from further developing.

Ensure the patient continues to believe that the problem is "out there" in the "broken system" rather than recognizing there is a problem with himself.

Keep up the good work,

Uncle Screwtape

So fight and argue about "people you've never met," and ignore the real issue that if you die in your sins tonight, without the saving grace of Jesus Christ's death as your payment, you will be lose much, much more than an election.

As Jesus Said, *"For what does it profit a man to gain the whole world and forfeit his soul?"*

Week 38:
His Business is Picking Up

"When you were dead in your transgressions and the uncircumcision of your flesh, He made you alive together with Him, having forgiven us all our transgressions, having canceled out the certificate of debt consisting of decrees against us, which was hostile to us; and He has taken it out of the way, having nailed it to the cross (Colossians 2:13-14)."

Riddle me this: *"Every Wednesday morning I appear, make it all disappear, including myself. What am I?"*

Another riddle, one every kid knows, may help you solve the first one. *"What has six wheels and flies?"*

Once a week we put out the trash, all the ugly and disgusting things we create in a week that no longer have any value. Then this stranger rolls up in a massive truck and makes it all go away. Presto-chango, we're clean again. Crazy? Not really.

Spiritually, Jesus is the Garbage-Man. If we let Him, He rolls up and takes away our ugly, smelly trash, our *"certificate of debt."* If He doesn't pick it up, then we have to deal with it ourselves. With no waste agreement our trash remains. Some think it's not a big pile; their trash isn't that smelly; never raped or killed; they're basically good.

But if you sin just once a day, after 70 years, your trashcan has 25,550 sins! Even a corrupt judge cannot ignore that record, but it's not the degree of the sin, or the volume, it's the fact that God is holy and His righteous character demands absolute perfection—holiness (Matthew 5:48, Habukkuk 1:13, James 2:10, Isaiah 59:2). God doesn't grade on a curve.

Our overflowing trashcan proves nobody's perfect, so holiness seems a cruel standard, but it is just to punish a lawbreaker. Sin must be punished, especially over 25,000 of them; otherwise God is a crooked judge (imagine if the MSU trial judge let Nassar go free after violating all those gymnasts).

Complicating this required justice and His standard of holiness is the fact that the Judge loves you, but He can't just wince at your trash if He's a good judge. Unless a full payment is made, He's stuck…loving a lawbreaker that He must condemn. And we're stuck too…how can anyone unholy pay the penalty for their own sin (Isaiah 64:6)?

Enter the Garbage-Man.

Jesus lived a sinless life to prove He was the perfect God-Man, and therefore qualified to pay our debt. An empty grave confirmed His death *"cancelled out the certificate of debt."* God's love and righteous judgment merged in Jesus, our substitute. His last words on the cross were *"It is finished,"* which also translates in Greek as *"paid in full."*

Ignoring His payment offer is like telling your garbage-man not to come back. Don't fool yourself that you're clean enough to face a holy God without your trash picked up. Your best effort still doesn't remove it. It's piling up at the bottom of your driveway now. Only the God-Man can *"take it out of the way,"* but His waste agreement is total surrender (Isaiah 1:18, Luke 6:46). Remember, God does not grade on a curve…He grades on a curb.

Week 39: Merry Christ!

"Things which eye has not seen and ear has not heard, and which have not entered the heart of man, all that God has prepared for those who love Him (1 Corinthians 2:9)."

Christmas is preparation. All *Boy Scouts* know to be prepared.

For weeks, I'd pore over a *Sears* catalog, preparing my Santa list to be perfect. It's a wondrous memory, recalling the gut-twisting joy that these toys might be under my tree! *"Tiny tots with their eyes all aglow"* was totally me as a child.

And how about you? If you could have anything now, what tops your list and makes it *"hard to sleep tonight?"*

A billion dollars; wisdom; an island in the Bahamas; President of the United States; a loved one resurrected? What would be your all-time top gift? For me, it's easy…really knowing God, personally, as my best friend (Jeremiah 9:23-24).

Imagine knowing the Creator of the universe–who made you, knows everything, can do anything, even give you those five things above–as your best friend. He's the absolute greatest gift.

If you agree, then I've got some real *"glad tidings,"* because it's possible (1 John 5:11-13). The carols we sing now, like *"God and sinners reconciled,"* reveal it all.

"Veiled in flesh the Godhead see, hail incarnate Deity." God became a man, but why? *"To ransom captive Israel"* and give us *"peace on Earth"* with complete forgiveness, through Jesus' life, death, and resurrection. But sin blocked this union, *"long lay the world, in sin and error pining,"* so He became sin and took our punishment (2 Corinthians 5:21).

His love and justice merged on the cross, and our Judge became our Father. God's friendship is under your tree right now (Romans 6:23)! So how do you get it?

You've practiced it every Christmas...just grab the gift...in simple faith, admit your sin, ask forgiveness, and change your attitude (God calls that repentance, changing your mind). Our attitude is conceit; we don't think we're that bad, or we're good enough as is, but then why did Jesus have to die?

In short, we don't get holiness.

God requires perfection, and clearly, nobody's perfect. Even one sin stops this relationship (James 2:10), and just "believing" mentally is not a saving repentance...even demons believe and they're not going to Heaven (James 2:19). So what do we do?

Real faith is action, but a meek action (grabbing this gift means genuine surrender). *"Where meek souls will receive Him still, the dear Christ enters in."* Repent, believe, and ask Jesus to "enter in" your body. God made a way, but His love isn't forced. He wants you to love Him, in humility to choose Christ, and put God back on top of your life.

Speaking of on top, did you know you top His list?

That's why He came...He loves you to death, literally. Even though you broke His heart, your repentance can be a thank you gift. *"Let every heart prepare Him room."* Christmas still means preparation, but in your heart, so please...take His gift and make Him a very Merry Christ!

Week 40: Inalienable

"And in the same region there were shepherds out in the field, keeping watch over their flock by night. And an angel of the Lord appeared to them, and the glory of the Lord shone around them, and they were filled with fear (Luke 2:8-9)."

Shepherds stink.

Passing a truckload of hogs in August, gives you some idea what shepherds absorb from months alone with their sheep. We've all sped past that semi-truck, eh?

And in Jesus' day, their character stunk even worse. According to theologian Joachim Jeremias, *"Most of the time they were dishonest and thieving; they led their herds onto other people's land and pilfered the produce of the land."*

A Hebrew Midrash on Psalm 23 reads, *"There is no more disreputable occupation than that of a shepherd."* Shepherds weren't accepted in court as witnesses because they were less than non-citizens, stuck on the bottom rung of Israel's social ladder.

The Mishnah refers to shepherds as *"incompetent,"* and another says no one should ever feel obligated to rescue a shepherd who has fallen into a pit. In short, they were considered sub-human. And yet, the Bethlehem angel came to them first.

In 1857, the U.S. Supreme Court ruled in the Dred Scott case, *"We think…that (black people) are not included, and were not intended to be included, under the word 'citizens' in the Constitution, and can therefore claim none of the rights and privileges which that instrument provides for and secures to citizens of the United States."* In short, they were considered sub-human and an estimated 10 million Africans died in transit. And yet, the Lord freed them from bondage after our Civil War.

The Nuremberg Laws of 1935 targeted Jews and declared that only those of German or related blood were eligible to be Reich citizens; the remainder were classed as state subjects, without citizenship rights. In short, they were considered sub-human and over 6 million were murdered. And yet, the Lord rescued them and they became a nation after a World War.

On March 29th, a new film is coming out called *Unplanned*. It's the true story of Abby Johnson, and the plight of another people group that today is considered sub-human like the shepherds, with no voice like the slaves, defenseless like the Jews, and without any rights as citizens. And yet, God cares about these outcasts too, even identifying as a shepherd Himself as Jeremias confirms, *"The rabbis ask with amazement how, in view of the despicable nature of shepherds, one can explain why God was called 'my shepherd' (Psalm 23)?"* Why a stinky outcast?

Because He chose to love the unloved, and enjoins us, *"You should defend those who cannot help themselves. Yes, speak up for the poor and helpless, and see that they get justice (Proverbs 31:8-9)."* Ironically, inalienable means, *"not subject to being taken away from,"* and yet our present injustice has taken away 61 million babies. If you saw what Abby saw, you'd defend their inalienable right to life, speak up for them, and see that they get justice, as would any Good Shepherd.

Week 41: Was Dead

"I was dead (Revelation 1:18)."

We were too late, but Joe was still warm.

Seeing someone dead, in this case my brother, is very unnerving. They look asleep, like at any moment they'll pull a Halloween prank and sit up, eyes wide, and shout, "BOO!" But he was really gone.

That hurt, bad. Still does today.

Later on, two funeral guys came and wheeled him out of his house with a flag draped over his body. That was so sad, so final, and so unstoppable. Two strangers took him, and Joe had no say in it. We stood and watched. Just watched…and cried.

Death won.

Jesus watched a dead man get carried out too, but He brought him back to life (Luke 7:11-17). I think on that in a more personal way now. He was dead. Not many people can say, *"Remember when I was dead?"* But…now…we all have a choice, a way out, because Jesus is *"the firstborn from the dead* (Colossians 1:18)."

Death is not the end.

Jesus came to end the death curse, restore us to God by cancelling our sin debt, so death is no longer winning because "was dead" is totally possible. Death lost! Though we will all die (Hebrews 9:27), and that death is from our sin, we can have empty graves just like Jesus (Colossians 2:13-14).

Often this column, *Religious Thoughts*, is situated next to the Obituaries. It's sobering for me to see that. Here are words of hope to defeat death, make peace with God, and live forever, placed right next to faces of our local dead.

Did they know, really know Jesus, and now see Him in person (2 Corinthians 5), or not (2 Thessalonians 1:8-9)?

Someday, you'll be wheeled out, your picture may be next to this column. How is it that you know you're taking this same trip and make no reservations? Friend, take some time and read the New Testament. Find a modern translation (like NASB, NIV, ESV, NLT) and read just two of the 27 books…the Gospel of John and Romans, and see if it rings true.

Read each book slowly, thoughtfully, and in one sitting. John's Gospel is only 21 short chapters; Romans is less, only 16 quick chapters. At the most, it will take you two hours. Two words that rarely go together, "was dead," hang in the balance, your balance.

But before you start, ask God to show you if this is true, if He's real, and if Jesus did in fact rise from the dead. That's it. Just ask Him to open your eyes, and see if His Spirit won't lead you to Himself.

The prophet Jeremiah wrote these inspired words in the Old Testament, *"If you look for Me wholeheartedly, you will find Me* (chapter 29, verse 13)."

That's a promise from God to you. If you really want to miss out on death, and say, "I was dead," then truly seeking Him will result in finding Him. He promised to reveal Himself to you. All it takes is a speck of faith to put death in your past…tense.

Week 42: Rock or Reek?

"For we are a fragrance of Christ to God among those who are being saved and among those who are perishing: to the one an aroma from death to death, to the other an aroma from life to life (2 Corinthians 2:14-16)."

Church stinks, so you probably skipped Easter, right?

Trust me, I get it. Christians do stink.

I remember ducking into my dorm room when I saw one coming down the hall at MSU. Something about Rob literally repelled me, like the Gettysburg battle stench in 1863. I avoided him.

"The field is covered with dead and wounded. Out here there is a stink unimaginable, it's definitely more than I thought when I signed up. All I wanted was an adventure and a little money at the age of 18, but now I'm figuring out that I've got to man up and get the job done if I want to survive. As I'm writing this there is very heavy firing to the right of me about 5 o'clock. By the sound of it it's coming right in our direction. I better get ready."

Just the thought of church probably gives you the Gettysburg Gag, a stink unimaginable. You've got good reasons too, like your spouse won't go, your job requires rest, golf or fishing, kid's activities, yard-work, your upbringing, the hypocrites, nice clothes, money-grubbers…there's just no time.

But did you ever wonder the real reason that you steer clear of church?

Your indifference to Him is exposed by their "stench," and that same repulsion I felt is really a warning that you're spiritually dead. Whiffing that smelly church in person on Sunday is like bursting in on your family breakfast and shouting, *"Who wants to go over to the funeral home with me? They just got some new bodies!"*

In short, a Christian's aroma (from life to life) reminds you of sin and death—your death and your sin (Romans 3:23, 6:23).

This "death to death" is not just your physical death or your spiritual deadness (Hebrews 9:27, Ephesians 2:1), but it's also your second eternal death...a separation from God if you ignore your sin.

A Christian is like smelling salts, a rancid alarm to wake you up from your coma, and to challenge your "good enough" indifference to Jesus. No one is truly good enough, and just one sin starts the death-stink. *"For whoever keeps the whole law and yet stumbles in one point, he has become guilty of all (James 2:10)."*

Friend, if you've sinned once, you're in danger. I know, I was too, but man up if you want to survive. Death is near, to the right at about 5 o'clock, and coming in your direction. You better get ready because it's bad news...you're guilty of all, a criminal, and perishing.

Thankfully, Easter's empty tomb proves the death problem is solved. Church isn't your issue; it's Jesus, the Rock of salvation. He died on your cross, and if you ignore that love then guess what really stinks. It's your choice. Rock or Reek?

Week 43: The Jesus Nut

"Those who trust in the Lord are as Mount Zion, which cannot be moved but abides forever (Psalm 125:1)."

Mountain peaks are never crowded.

That's probably true because genuine trust is a rare commodity, and in alpine climbing you are putting your life in the hands of your partner, some rope, and a few metal spikes to secure against certain death. Visiting Lauterbrunnen, Switzerland made me curious about the sport.

I've been reading about the fabled *Eiger* in the Swiss Alps (13,015 feet) and the first attempts to climb its deadly North Face in the 1930's. In doing so, I learned a new word (always splendid fun for a writer)…belay.

I've heard "belay" before, as in nautical terms when a superior officer countermands an order with, *"Belay that order, Ensign!"* But "belay" in mountain climbing jargon means that someone is providing support to a climber who is trying to move up the mountain. They are an anchor-of-safety in case the other climber falls, a life-saving stopgap measure (they are tied to each other's waist).

It's interesting that the Psalmist listed Mount Zion as a simile for trusting in the Lord.

Mount Zion is the biblical mountain where Abraham sacrificed his son Isaac, and the spot that David purchased to build Jerusalem. In the Bible, it is equated with complete and absolutely guaranteed unshakable trust.

Jerusalem has been conquered and destroyed many times, but Mount Zion abides forever. I have stood in the tunnels under Jerusalem on the very bedrock of Mount Zion and touched the bus-sized foundation stones that the famous Wailing Wall rests upon above.

It will never fall.

The Bible, however, says that we have already fallen, *"for all have sinned and fall short of the glory of God* (Romans 3:23)." Spiritually, our rope has snapped and we are plunging to our death, *"...you were dead in your trespasses and sin* (Ephesians 2:1)."

But if we trust in Him, we are as secure as Mount Zion. If you're not sure that your trust is a genuine, eternal, and saving Mount Zion faith, then consider the Jesus Nut.

The "Jesus Nut" was a giant stainless-steel nut that attached the main rotor blades to the body on the first helicopter. According to the 1939 inventor, Igor Sikorsky, if that nut failed then *"the next person you see will be Jesus."* But it is also known in climbing circles as a crucial extra piece of gear above the belay anchor that will save both climbers in case the lead climber falls.

Frankly, you'd be nuts not to have a Jesus Nut on your rope because biblically speaking you've already fallen and without Jesus as your belay, you will perish (Romans 6:23). Let Him be your partner while you climb up.

If you're at the end of your rope, call out to Him today and He will stop your fall, as it says in 2 Corinthians 6:2, " *'AT THE ACCEPTABLE TIME I LISTENED TO YOU, AND ON THE DAY OF SALVATION I HELPED YOU.' Behold, now is 'THE ACCEPTABLE TIME,' behold, now is 'THE DAY OF SALVATION.'"*

Week 44: Guns and Butter

"So teach us to number our days that we may get a heart of wisdom (Psalm 90:12)."

I don't recall much from my Economics class at MSU except that our Professor wore a Hawaiian shirt when he taught us, my final grade was a measly 1.5, and if you spend all your assets on guns, then you can't buy butter.

In other words, assets are limited and they cannot be used twice. If you spend it all on butter, then no guns. Basic economics.

The same goes for our non-renewable days, which if you live to be 70 years old then you'll have about 25,000 days to spend…days you will use up by keeping yourself busy until you come to the end of your days. Most of us use up those days at work, sleeping, raising a family, or hobbies on weekends.

Like a dollar spent, they are gone forever.

The Bible says we should think hard about those remaining days, number them, if we want to be wise, but no one does. Not really. We just jump on the hamster wheel and run. Maybe it'd help if we had a visual reminder, like thousands of marbles in a jar on our dresser that each morning we took one marble out and put it in our pocket.

Maybe that would help us use our days more wisely when we realize how short and valuable they are and use them being kind, volunteering, spending time with our kids, etc. Maybe, but I think there's a better way.

Think back to when you were a child and the *"What would you wish for if a genie granted you three wishes?"* moment.

Every kid knows the third wish is to have a million more wishes, right? I think that's what God may be getting at here with numbering our days to have a heart of wisdom.

It's not necessarily investing the 25,000 days correctly by camping with your kids or joining the Peace Corps, but realizing there is an end…a guns and butter moment where the days are all spent. Then what?

The answer is obvious…just make more days.

Make your third wish count by living forever…by getting serious about Jesus Christ. His death and resurrection is that third wish to make a million more wishes. Remember what He said when His friend Lazarus died in chapter 11 of the Gospel of John?

"I am the resurrection and the life. The one who believes in Me will live, even though they die; and whoever lives by believing in me will never die."

Catch that? Even though you die (use up all your days), you can get more days by believing in Jesus.

But believing isn't acknowledging He existed; it's giving up your remaining days to Him as your Lord. You trade your remaining days by surrendering all of them to Him so you can live forever (the third wish). Just ask Him to forgive you for all your stupid days (sin), literally come into your body, and take over as Lord.

Week 45: How did you know...?

"These things I have written to you who believe in the name of the Son of God, so that you may know that you have eternal life (1 John 5:13)."

I love movies, especially if it's based on a true story. Truth is stranger than Fiction.

A favorite is the Oscar winning *"Papillon"* with Steve McQueen as Henri Charriere, a convicted murderer who wrote about his imprisonment in French Guiana's penal colonies.

Papillon (butterfly in French and Henri's nickname from his tattoo) spent 14 years there and escaped eight times.

My favorite scene is when Papillon escapes and tries to get a boat from a leper colony. The leper leader is reluctant to help an outsider and tests Steve, who cannot bear to look at his disfigured face.

> *"Why don't you have the courtesy to look at me when you speak?" he asks.*
>
> *Papillon raises his eyes to see a horrific face sucking on a cigar.*
>
> *"Do you like cigars?"*
>
> *"When I can get 'em," Papillon says.*
>
> *"Try this one."*
>
> *The leper offers his gooey cigar and Steve puffs on it, and then hands it back.*
>
> *"How did you know I have dry leprosy, and it isn't contagious?"*
>
> *McQueen replies, "I didn't."*

This scene is the quintessential example of genuine faith. Steve acts on his belief.

It isn't head knowledge or something he just says he believes. He does it. Papillon steps out in faith and tugs on a gooey cigar that had just been on those rotting lips. He took a chance and acted on his belief that freedom was worth the risk of leprosy.

Real faith, a real saving-eternal faith, is like that. It involves action. If your faith in Jesus is genuine, then you'll act on it publicly (like getting baptized, for instance).

But if you're not 100% sure about Heaven, you don't have to take a chance like Papillon. The Bible says you can be absolutely certain, and that's precisely why it was written:

"And the testimony is this, that God has given us eternal life, and this life is in His Son. He who has the Son has the life; he who does not have the Son of God does not have the life. These things I have written to you who believe in the name of the Son of God, so that you may know that you have eternal life (1 John 5:11-13)."

Do you think God would make something as critical as your salvation hard to understand when it cost Him His only son? He wants you to get it, figuratively and literally. If you're not 100% sure, try reading the New Testament.

Ironically, McQueen led a wild life with fast cars, motorcycles, and heavy partying, but six months before he died Steve got it… and accepted Christ! He wanted to know for sure, and when he understood the Bible's message of salvation, a free gift, the King of Cool knelt before the King of Kings.

How cool is that? And the good news is you can know too, and as an added bonus…you can meet Steve McQueen!

Week 46:
My Blind Mom, Plus Nothing

"And Jesus said, 'For judgment I came into this world, so that those who do not see may see, and that those who see may become blind (John 9:39).'"

My mom was legally blind.

When she was 18, while sitting in church, her left eye went black, like a dark curtain descended.

Can you imagine the terror?

The doctor said it was from a recent bout with Scarlet Fever. After several painful and unsuccessful operations, and a very long stay at *Wills Eye Hospital* in Philadelphia, she decided to just live with a detached retina. Over the years, her right eye became strained and badly weakened.

I grew up helping her to see price tags, clothing sizes, bus stops, addresses, ingredients, and even people. It was normal for me to be her eyes and when I turned 16 she was my excuse to get to drive our family car as her chauffeur. Being blind was our normal.

Late in life, after going to church every Sunday, she finally realized religion wasn't the answer. After teaching Sunday school, serving in the Altar Guild, and regular attendance, she still had no assurance of going to Heaven when she died.

Then one day she heard Dr. J. Vernon McGee's "Thru the Bible" radio program, and after he explained the gospel, she became a genuine believer! Although still physically blind, the eyes of her heart were opened and her life changed (Ephesians 1:18).

In John's ninth chapter, Jesus heals a blind man who later believes in Him, but the religious experts did not believe He was God-in-the-flesh. They could physically see Him, but they were blind spiritually to His true identity.

These Pharisees, who had memorized major portions of the Old Testament in order to obey over 600 written laws, and oral traditions that they made up, thought they were righteous because of what they did.

But Jesus told them they were blind.

They had missed the point, which was Jesus Himself (Deuteronomy 18:15, Isaiah 53, John 5:39-47). They scoffed at His claim to be God, the Son of Man, because He healed on the Sabbath and violated one of their most holy rules not to work on the Sabbath. So what's the point?

If you're reading this then you're not blind, but are you blind spiritually?

If you think doing things (like the Pharisees) or church activities (like my mom) makes you right with God, you've missed the point of Jesus too. Consider "doing" versus "dying," and Galatians 2:21 that says, *"If righteousness comes through the Law, then Christ died needlessly."* In other words, His death was worthless.

Thanks to McGee, my blind mom "saw" the truth of the gospel, plus nothing. If you're not seeing Jesus, not 100% certain of Heaven, then maybe you need some J. Vernon too. Luckily, his "Thru the Bible" chats are still available online, but he no longer has any faith.

He stopped using it on December 1, 1988 when he saw Jesus face to face, just like my mom who now sees Him perfectly too. Can you imagine their joy?

Week 47: Myopic or Himopic?

"...take your ease, eat, drink, and be merry (Luke 12:16-21)."

In the 80's, Steve Taylor sang *"What is the Measure of Your Success?"*

Most base success on stuff that doesn't transfer into eternity… home, possessions, income, savings, education, looks, job, spouse, car, fame, personality, strength, title, family, talent, or intellect. We quietly boast in these, but it all stays when we leave.

Jesus warned that this "success" is shortsighted, even foolish. True success involves God and souls. *"Then He said to them, 'Beware, and be on your guard against every form of greed; for not even when one has an abundance does his life consist of his possessions.'*

"And He told them a parable, saying, 'The land of a rich man was very productive. And he began reasoning to himself, saying, 'What shall I do, since I have no place to store my crops?' Then he said, 'This is what I will do: I will tear down my barns and build larger ones, and there I will store all my grain and my goods. And I will say to my soul, 'Soul, you have many goods laid up for many years to come; take your ease, eat, drink and be merry.'

"But God said to him, 'You fool! This very night your soul is required of you; and now who will own what you have prepared?' So is the man who stores up treasure for himself, and is not rich toward God.'"

Jeremiah described true success, something worth bragging about (chapter 9): *"Thus says the Lord, 'Let not a wise man boast of his wisdom, and let not the mighty man boast of his might, let not a rich man boast of his riches; but let him who boasts boast of this, that he understands and knows Me, that I am the Lord who exercises lovingkindness, justice and righteousness on earth; for I delight in these things,' declares the Lord."*

Getting to know a person starts with learning what they think.

Have you ever seriously read the Bible to see what God thinks? It says that He loves you (John 3:1-21), but your sin separates you from Him (Isaiah 59:2) and your good deeds stink (Isaiah 64:6). We're so infected with sin that we can't be near Him (Habakkuk 1:13), and we're criminals (Romans 3:9-23) awaiting His justice (Nahum 1:3).

So until your sin is removed, you cannot know and understand Him (Ephesians 2:1). Sadly, because of sin we're fixated on ourselves, shortsighted, My-opic, but we should be Him-opic, focused on Him. But how do we do that?

You've probably never heard of Steve Taylor, but knowing of Steve Taylor is not the same as knowing him, personally. Knowing of Jesus isn't the same as knowing Him either, but reading the Bible is how to know Him and His solution (2 Corinthians chapter 5). Stuff stays, but a soul transfers into eternity, so redeeming a soul is true success, being rich toward God. So let's start there…with your soul. Are you sure you know Jesus? If not, I'd love to introduce you to see how great He is.

Week 48:
Can You Trust the Bible?

"This is the judgment, that the Light has come into the world, and men loved the darkness rather than the Light, for their deeds were evil (John 3:19)."

The phaonmneal pweor of the huamn mnid, aoccdrnig to Cmabrigde Uinervtisy rsceeacrh, syas it deosn't mttaer in waht oredr the ltteers in a wrod are arnarged, the olny iprmoatnt tihng is taht the fsirt and lsat ltteer be in the rghit pclae.

The rset can be a taotl mses and you wlil sltil raed it wouthit a porbelm.

Tihs is bcuseae the huamn mnid deos not raed ervey lteter, but the wrod as a wlohe.

Amzanig, huh? Bleeive me?

Our nepswaper clumon lsat mnoth daelt wtih the autthoiry of the Blbie and wehtehr or not God wluod alolw sotehming as criitcal as His supneraturlaly reealved insrtucnstios to us for our etnreal savlaiton bieng oepn to consfuion, tapmernig, or miinsterprteatoin. Eevn in tihs prupesfluly miexd up cloumn, we stlil get the mian piont of tihs mesasge.

How mcuh mroe so if the Amligthy God watned to comumniacte His soltuion for our suols to dael with sin and detah? Wulod God alolw any ctnoamiantion to His mesasge? Wloud He mkae it hrad to unedrtasnd? Is He pwoerufl enuogh to ptroect His wrods?

Thsee are obivosuly rhetocrial qusteions. Of coruse God is storng enoguh to procett His svlaation meassge. The rael quetison is actulaly a mattetr of the haert...are you wlliing to reveice His measgse by rediang the Bilbe for yosruelf?

Look waht Jeuss siad in Luke 16:31, "But He said to him, 'If they do not listen to Moses and the Prophets, they will not be persuaded even if someone rises from the dead.'" If tehy wolud not acecpt the messgae of the Old Tetsamnet rergading tiehr sin and His lvoe for tehm, eevn afetr sieeng so mnay demontsratoins of His mirauclous lvoe, eevn rasiing the daed wluod not sotfen tehir hrad heatrs. It's not crebidility…it's stubbnroess.

Your hrad herat, lvoe of slef, and sin, preevnts you form eevn reanidg His Wrod. So lte's hvae no mroe excsues abuot the Bbile bieng flul of conrtadicitons or mistinerprteatoins. The rael isuse is yuor haert and you simlpy dno't lvoe God.

Or myabe yuo're afarid, like a naghuty chlid who feras dispciline, but tihs is precilsey why Jeuss cmae…to tkae yuor puhnisment, so you colud cmoe bcak. Lkie the Prdoigal Son stroy taht Jseus tlod in Luke 15, yuor Fatehr lnogs for you to cmoe hmoe.

Wlil you gvie up and adimt yuor need (Isaiah 64:6), or mkae lmae exucses aoubt the Bilbe's inipsration. Hvae you eevn seriolsuy raed the Bblie? Why not try rdaeing the Gospel of John and see for yruoslef if Jeuss is the olny way as He clamied (John 14:6)? You mgiht fnid taht He loevs you, and olny watns to hlep you. Eevn miexd up, lkie this cloumn, if yuo'll just raed His Wrod you may fnid taht He loevs you. If not, tehn mabye yuo're the rael contracidtion for criticizing soemthing yuo've not seirously reda and it's not the Blibe…or pehraps you jsut lvoe the dkraness?

Week 49: God in Skin!

"Therefore the Lord Himself will give you a sign: Behold, a virgin will be with child and bear a son, and she will call His name Immanuel (Isaiah 7:14)."

Sometimes familiarity makes it hard to see the astounding.

Hard to believe, but living next to the Grand Canyon can eventually become ho-hum. We sometimes have that "canyon problem" with Christmas too. Read that verse from Isaiah again, but this time very, very, slowly. Go ahead. I'll wait. Really, I will.

About 2,700 years before Linus explained Christmas to Charlie Brown, Isaiah predicted a sign would be given to solve our sin problem. It baffled the Jews…a sinful human (who never had sex) would birth a God-baby? In Hebrew *Immanuel* means, "God with us."

God in skin! That's some sign!

As amazing as that is, even kinda' crazy, we realize now there was no other logical way to save us, but some still miss God's Grand Canyon in Bethlehem. Christmas has become too commonplace. Perhaps a glimpse into the Sign-giver's conundrum will jolt your Christmas spirit with the supernatural crackle it so richly deserves.

Consider the problem:

1. Nobody's perfect. God knows we've made mistakes and done wrong (Romans 3:23).

2. God is just. His righteousness demands an accounting for every wrong (Nahum 1:3).

3. God is holy. He must execute justice to be a good and fair judge (Habakkuk 1:13).

4. God loves us. We're guilty, a death penalty, but a God-Man steps in (Romans 5:6-10).

Incarnation was the only logical solution for balancing His love, justice, holiness, and our sin. God in skin, a drastic measure, bridged the spiritual chasm our sin created between us (Isaiah 59:2).

Matthew then names Isaiah's God-baby, *"'She will bear a Son; and you shall call His name Jesus, for He will save His people from their sins.' Now all this took place to fulfill what was spoken by the Lord through the prophet (Isaiah): Behold, the virgin shall be with child and shall bear a Son, and they shall call His name Immanuel, which translated means, 'God with us.'"*

Jesus means "Jehovah saves" in Hebrew.

And Micah identifies His birth location, *"...as for you Bethlehem... one will go forth for Me to be ruler in Israel, his goings forth are from long ago, from the days of eternity."* An eternal king, "God with us," will come from Bethlehem named "Jehovah saves." God and skin merged at Bethlehem; love and justice merged at Jerusalem's cross (Isaiah 53).

And God told this to Micah 700 years beforehand. That's some serious crackle!

Bethlehem is God gifting Himself to you for free (Romans 6:23). Who works for a Christmas gift? You simply take it, but His present has even more crackle—it makes you as righteous as God Himself (2 Corinthians 5:21)! This is Christmas…God in skin…removing sin… to make you as holy as Him…to reunite us. That's some Merry.

Canyon problem solved, the just for the unjust. It's crazy-love-logic, but if that's too hard to believe, then maybe just skin that gift and see for yourself (John 1:12). Go ahead. I'll wait.

Week 50: Remember When...?

"God raised Him up again, putting an end to the agony of death...(Acts 2:24)."

I don't remember reading this verse in the Book of Acts.

I know I have, it's underlined in my Bible, but it never hit me like it did until today. It's the whole Bible, in just 13 words. Pretty succinct, eh?

At 60, I'm more forgetful, waxing nostalgic more and more, especially kid memories—building forts, rock fights, baseball games every day, trees climbed to scary heights, or playing Three Wishes…get a million bucks, meet Al Kaline, and become an astronaut.

But now, as an adult, if we're honest, what we really want is to cheat death, to be able to say, *"Hey, remember when…I was dead?"* Our death in the past tense (was dead). Doubt it? I'll prove it with your own Yes and No, respectively, to my next two questions.

First, think you'll die someday? And, knowing that you will die, do you think about it much? That's odd. You know you'll die, but you avoid considering the afterlife. Why?

Solomon said, *"It's better to go to funerals than parties because death is the end of every man and the living take it to heart* (Ecclesiastes 7:2)."

Funerals force you to ponder what you won't think about…a kind of warning light. And Jesus, who cheated death, proving He was God in the flesh, is also something we avoid giving any serious consideration. See a weird pattern here? We ignore our biggest problem and Jesus, the only solution.

For some reason, we do not want to think about our death, or consider the one person who ended death when "God raised Him up again." Can you explain that avoidance? There are a lot of answers, but I'll throw one out from my own childhood. Fear!

One day, I got caught stealing some pretty significant items and I hid from my Father, knowing full well he'd punish me (and rightfully so). I hid in the basement under our pool table. I had to return the items, and it was embarrassing, but I cannot remember him punishing me. My fear was unfounded.

The next day I was still his son! Nothing changed, and for 70 more years he was my Dad. He never mentioned it ever, and loved a thief.

I submit that you know you're guilty too, fear your Heavenly Father will punish you, and so you avoid facing Him…ignorance is bliss, but if your car's brakes are broken you can be ignorant, in bliss, and dead. Your brake light, like a funeral, is a warning to respond.

I further submit that you're wrong about our Heavenly Father, just as I was about my Dad. *"For God so loved the world* (that's you, guilty), *that He gave His only begotten Son, that whoever* (you again) *believes in Him should not perish, but have eternal life."*

Twenty-five words to say He loves you, almost twice those in Acts 2:24, which should make you think twice about responding. Repent, believe and He'll forgive you, and then 150 years from now you can wax nostalgic with, *"Hey, remember when…I was dead?"*

Week 51: Wrecognized

"And He said, 'Truly I say to you, no prophet is welcome in his hometown (Luke 4:24).'"

"Wait! I know that guy! What movie did I see him in? Ah, this is gonna' bug me."

As a screenwriter, I'm always trying to recognize a familiar looking actor in a movie from a former role, trying to recall where I saw them before. It wrecks me when I can't identify the actor when I know I know them so well.

When Jesus came back home to Nazareth where He was brought up, well known by everyone as Joseph's son, the kid around the corner, no one recognized Him for who He really was…the long-awaited Messiah! They knew of Him…but didn't know Him.

Granted, spotting the Creator-in-the-flesh, literally, is a bit new for sure, but how strange that those who knew Him so well, intimately, who were so used to Him, so familiar with Him, didn't recognize Him?

We have that same myopia here in America. Jesus is so well known, that we ignore Him. Most of us have grown up in a church and heard His name almost daily. We know Jesus inside and out. We are very familiar with Him, so much so that we don't actually know Him. The "kid around the corner." We politely ignore Him.

I was in Israel three weeks ago on a writing assignment for the *Israel Ministry of Tourism* and stood in the very place where Luke chapter 4 records Jesus' miracles in His local synagogue in Capernaum (v.23). It was a chilling experience to stand where He stood!

Another thing amazed me in Israel. Everywhere you go there are Orthodox Jews who still do not recognize Jesus as the Messiah. They study the Torah for 14 hours a day, phylacteries wrapped on their heads and arms, praying daily (even on our flight), inspecting ingredient labels to eat only Kosher foods, dressed in black, trying to keep their 613 commandments, with long peyots and beards, etc.

Truly impressive devotion!

Look at what Matthew recorded in chapter 15 about Jesus' reaction to those who professed to knowing God, who were experts in His Law, who saw Him face to face, knew His name, and still missed the point:

"You hypocrites, rightly did Isaiah prophesy of you:

'THIS PEOPLE HONORS ME WITH THEIR LIPS,

BUT THEIR HEART IS FAR AWAY FROM ME.

'BUT IN VAIN DO THEY WORSHIP ME,

TEACHING AS DOCTRINES THE PRECEPTS OF MEN.'"

Just because you put a mouse in a cookie jar, it doesn't make him a cookie. Don't assume because you know of Him, that you know Him. Crack open the New Testament and meet the Man who stood in Capernaum. I bet you won't recognize Him.

Week 52: Sick of Christmas

"Veiled in flesh the Godhead see: hail the incarnate Deity, pleased as man with man to dwell, Jesus our Emmanuel."

Charles Wesley wrote those words in 1739 for a Christmas day hymn, *"Hark! The Herald Angels Sing."*

The astonishing truth of what he wrote is sung every December with gusto around the world. It even made it into the best Christmas film ever, *"It's A Wonderful Life."* Specifically, that God miraculously took on human form, which makes complete sense if God (a Spirit) wants to relate to us (flesh).

I mean, if God wanted to communicate with ants, he'd become an ant, right?

But many people are sick of Christmas. Consider this actual Scrooge-like take on Christmas: *"How long do we have to put up with this? I used to like Christmas when I was a kid, but now it just gets to be a drag. It's just commercialism and nonsense now. What's the point?"*

Can you relate to that Charlie Brown-like query too? If it's true for you, then you missed the point, and you'd do well to listen to Linus' famous answer from the Bible again (Luke 2:8-14). His answer is Jesus' birth, *"veiled in flesh, the Godhead see,"* and it's an epiphany! If you don't see God-in-the-flesh in Christmas, *"our Emmanuel,"* then Christmas is a drag.

But if Jesus is Who He said He was, as the Old Testament prophecies foretold (almost 400 of them!), and proved it by rising from the dead, then Christmas is the most historic event ever (before the resurrection)! It's impossible some say, but they probably have not investigated from the Bible what Wesley's Carol proclaims. The mystery of Christmas, and in it not being a drag, is in discovering who this baby was in Bethlehem.

Doyle's master of solving a mystery, Sherlock Holmes, said *"when you have eliminated the impossible, whatever remains, however improbable, must be the truth."* There's not room here to make a complete proof for his Deity, but consider chapter 5 in Micah and John. No one has any control over where they will be born, unless they are God. The prophet Micah wrote this over 700 years before Jesus was born, referring to the birth of an eternal ruler in a tiny town in Israel:

"But as for you, Bethlehem Ephrathah, too little to be among the clans of Judah, from you One will go forth for Me to be ruler in Israel. His goings forth are from long ago, from the days of eternity."

Jesus said as much to the Jews in John 5:39, *"You diligently study the Scriptures because you think that by them you possess eternal life. These are the Scriptures that testify about Me."* And again in verse 46, *"For if you believed in Moses, you would believe Me, for he wrote of Me."*

Jesus either lied, was crazy, or He was God. *"Word of the Father, now in flesh appearing. O come let us adore Him."* That'll cure your Christmas sickness.

Appendix I – Bonus Weeks

Bonus Week 1: Over 700 Years Before Gettysburg

"I am God, and there is no other; I am God, and there is none like me. I make known the end from the beginning, from ancient times, what is still to come (Isaiah 46:9-10)."

On November 19, 1863, Lincoln's Gettysburg Address explained the entire Civil War's significance with just 272 words. A miraculous feat, but Lincoln's perfect speech pales beside Isaiah's 405 words in chapter 53 (below). Why?

Because Isaiah wrote them 700 years before Jesus' crucifixion!

Who has believed what he has heard from us? And to whom has the arm of the Lord been revealed? For he grew up before him like a young plant, and like a root out of dry ground; he had no form or majesty that we should look at him, and no beauty that we should desire him.

He was despised and rejected by men, a man of sorrows and acquainted with grief; and as one from whom men hide their faces he was despised, and we esteemed him not. Surely he has borne our griefs and carried our sorrows; yet we esteemed him stricken, smitten by God, and afflicted.

But he was pierced for our transgressions; he was crushed for our iniquities; upon him was the chastisement that brought us peace, and with his wounds we are healed. All we like sheep have gone astray; we have turned—every one—to his own way; and the Lord has laid on him the iniquity of us all.

He was oppressed, and he was afflicted, yet he opened not his mouth; like a lamb that is led to the slaughter, and like a sheep that before its shearers is silent, so he opened not his mouth. By oppression and judgment he was taken away; and as for his generation, who considered that he was cut off out of the land of the living, stricken for the transgression of my people?

And they made his grave with the wicked and with a rich man in his death, although he had done no violence, and there was no deceit in his mouth. Yet it was the will of the Lord to crush him; he has put him to grief; when his soul makes an offering for guilt, he shall see his offspring; he shall prolong his days; the will of the Lord shall prosper in his hand.

Out of the anguish of his soul he shall see and be satisfied; by his knowledge shall the righteous one, my servant, make many to be accounted righteous, and he shall bear their iniquities. Therefore I will divide him a portion with the many, and he shall divide the spoil with the strong, because he poured out his soul to death and was numbered with the transgressors; yet he bore the sin of many, and makes intercession for the transgressors.

Imagine if Gettysburg was predicted with this detail in 1163. Impossible you say, unless *"I am God and there is no other,"* saw Gettysburg (and the crucifixion) 700 years beforehand! Which if He did, it also means He knew you'd read this today, and your response to Isaiah 53:1. What say you? *"Who has believed what he has heard from us?"*

Bonus Week 2: Still Celebrating Christmas?

"...and hope does not disappoint, because the love of God has been poured out within our hearts through the Holy Spirit who was given to us (Romans 5:5)."

Sometimes when the holidays end we experience a bit of an emotional downer; that rosy carol-infested time of yuletide bliss gives way to just a cold and dreary January fizzle.

Well, there's a way to keep that same holiday hope permanently flaming, as when Scrooge's nephew Fred says it to be,

"…a kind, forgiving, charitable, pleasant time; the only time I know of, in the long calendar of the year, when men and women seem by one consent to open their shut-up hearts freely, and to think of people below them as if they really were fellow-passengers to the grave, and not another race of creatures bound on other journeys."

Or as Scrooge puts it so succinctly after his spirited conversion,

"I will honour Christmas in my heart, and try to keep it all the year. I will live in the Past, the Present, and the Future. The Spirits of all Three shall strive within me. I will not shut out the lessons that they teach."

Without the Person of Christmas, in our heart, our hearts are shut up tight. Keeping Christmas, maintaining that joy of the Incarnation of Bethlehem, means inviting Him into your heart…permanently.

As Paul says, in Romans 5:5, in order to have that *"hope that does not disappoint,"* God's love must enter your heart in the gift of *"the Holy Spirit who was given to us."* That's what Jesus meant when He said that we must be born again in John chapter three,

Now there was a man of the Pharisees, named Nicodemus, a ruler of the Jews; this man came to Jesus by night and said to Him, "Rabbi, we know that You have come from God as a teacher; for no one can do these signs that You do unless God is with Him."

Jesus answered and said to him, "Truly, truly, I say to you, unless one is born again he cannot see the kingdom of God."

Nicodemus said to Him, "How can a man be born when he is old? He cannot enter a second time into his mother's womb and be born, can he?"

Jesus answered, "Truly, truly, I say to you, unless one is born of water and the Spirit he cannot enter into the kingdom of God."

Everyone is born physically, when your mom's water breaks. That is the first birth, by water. The second is what Scrooge experienced, a spiritual change of heart where you are born a second time by the Holy Spirit entering your heart.

The key to keeping Christmas all the year is in having Jesus inside of your body, literally inside of you, in the form of the Holy Spirit. That's what makes you a Christian…when you open your shut-up heart to the Holy Spirit to come inside of you. It's also what makes Christmas a daily celebration all year.

Bonus Week 3: Hasenpfeffer Hostage

"You fool! This very night your soul is demanded of you (Luke 12:20)."

Why is God so concerned with Death? The Bible mentions Death 372 times, so you could say God cares about it a lot, even that He's obsessed with it. Since Halloween is only a week away it seemed like a good time to talk about our demise, like the dinner caught in our fence last week, it can be scary.

Our dinner was disguised as a rabbit, his front half outside of the fence with two feet on the ground. His back legs were up in the air inside the fence, firmly stuck at his hips (which were rubbed raw and exposed from struggling to get free). He was stuck all night.

As I approached him the spiritual imagery was deafening; he was just like us. Stuck, helpless, and dying. He needed to be rescued. The Bible says we are spiritually dead and need rescuing too (Ephesians 2:1-5). We tend to ignore our plight, that is until a funeral arrives (Ecclesiastes 7:1-2), which like an alarm clock, wakes us up to our appointment.

So what is Death exactly? The Bible says, *"The wages of sin is death."* If you work at Sin, Inc. then your paycheck will be Death (Romans 6:23). In the Bible, Sin and Death are linked together and you are fully employed as members of the human race.

• Death is physical and spiritual. *"The soul that sins shall surely die* (Ezekiel 18:20)."

• Universal. *"All have sinned and fall short of the glory of God* (Romans 3:23)."

• Divisive. *"Your sins have made a separation between you and your God* (Isaiah 59:2)."

• Inescapable. *"It is appointed for men to die once, and after this comes judgment* (Hebrews 9:27)."

• Finished. Jesus killed Death for all of us by rising from the dead, but we have to accept His help (1 Corinthians 15:24-26; John 1:12). Your death sentence can be pardoned.

But without Jesus, like my rabbit, you're stuck…separated. I could have shot the rabbit (the fence was to protect our apple tree), but out of mercy I freed the thief. Are you exhausted, rubbed raw with guilt, the fear of death, and judgment? Jesus offers mercy, release from your offenses. *"But God demonstrates His own love toward us in that while we were yet sinners* (stuck rabbits), *Christ died for us* (Romans 5:8)."

So why is God so obsessed with our Death problem? The answer is in another word in the Bible, mentioned 541 times. God is also obsessed with the word Love…for you, to the point of His own death to rescue you from it, if you want His help (John 3:16).

Bonus Week 4: Breadcrumbs in the Sky

"When I consider Thy heavens, the work of Thy fingers (Psalm 8)."

Two college roommates disagreed on the origin of the universe. Bob was a diehard Evolutionist, while Jerry was a devout Christian who believed in Creation. Despite their different worldviews, they remained good friends and both respected true Science.

They agreed that Evolution and Creation were theories, and not a fact since Science is based on two main pillars—Observation and Repetition. Since no one was there to observe the birth of the Universe, and no one could repeat it, both were only theories.

After going round and round, they concluded that both theories required faith in the vast circumstantial evidence. Beyond that, they were deadlocked. They saw the evidences through their own bias. The Evolutionist got behind in his classes because of a family emergency and had to go home often, and so Jerry tried to help him with his assignments.

Bob's World Geography 403 class was especially challenging and being gone for several weeks meant he was flunking in his major's most important class for graduation. Only acing his final project, worth 75% of his final grade, could save him, so Jerry looked over his friend's syllabus, and secretly got to work.

He made a huge globe out of papier-mâché to the exact scale with three dimensional topography, mountain ranges, oceans, and all the major rivers. Jerry hand-painted the Earth, labeled the continents, identified each country, and all their capital cities. As an Electrical Engineering major, he even wired it inside to light up these cities so that at night you could see it. It was magnificent, and even more stunning in the dark!

When Bob got back to the dorm, he saw the amazing work his friend had done for him over the last three weeks. Jerry closed the blinds, and it streamed from within like a giant ballroom chandelier. Bob was speechless, flabbergasted, but finally he had to know.

"Where did this come from?" he asked, seeing his name and class on the globe's base.

"You won't believe it, but while you were gone the paper, the wire, the glue, the electrical wires, and all the paint just appeared here in our room one day. So I put it in a pile in the center of our room and shocked it with electricity every day, for 24 hours, for the last three weeks. When I woke up this morning, there it was! A miracle! Something out of nothing, I can't believe it, but I guess Darwin was right."

His stunned friend didn't say anything. Bob looked mad. Finally, he went to the window, opened the blinds and looked out at the storm clouds moving off, changing into a beautiful blue sky, and then Bob admitted, *"Intelligent design implies...."*

"Implies a Designer," Jerry said smiling, and gave him the receipts for his materials. *"You owe the designer $74.87, and maybe even reconsider the work of His fingers?"*

Bonus Week 5: The Christmas Psalm

"And He will redeem Israel from all his iniquities (Psalm 130:8)."

How does Psalm 130 relate to celebrating the story of a Jewish baby's birth in Israel over 2,000 years ago? Good question. Let's look at a few choice words to see God's plot.

The Hebrew word here for "redeem" is *padah*, which means to ransom or release, what we would define as "an outsider intervening to free someone from a bad situation." We've all seen the movie, the rich parent gives up millions to get their kidnapped child back. That's Hollywood, but God's Christmas storyline is much more real, and personal.

From beyond Eternity, viewing Earth from God's perspective, you are that child, being held captive by unseen chains, and God is dropping off a bagful of cash. At this time of year, a favorite Christmas carol comes to mind when we talk about a "ransom."

"O Come, O Come, Emmanuel…and ransom captive Israel, that mourns in lonely exile here, until the Son of God appears," a desperate plea for God to come and rescue us, but from what? *"Long lay the world in sin and error pining."* Our own sin and judgment.

This baby is God Himself, disguised in flesh and blood, who pierced Time and Space, for one purpose…our reclamation, an old Dickens-like word defined as "the process of claiming something back, or of reasserting a right," like saving Ebenezer Scrooge's soul.

Jesus did just that…He came in fulfillment of the Old Testament prophecies to rescue Israel, to take back His own who were in exile, held captive by sin, powerless to stop a horrible outcome––a righteous judgment on our sin. Thankfully, God loves not only Israel, but all of us too. This is the Christmas story, a story of a helpless child being held captive and then rescued by another Child who dies for us. Psalm 130 lays it all out.

Read it for yourself, and then consider His Christmas gift to redeem your own soul.

- A desperate, nowhere to turn cry for help (verses 1-2).

- Our chains of sin binding us, and preventing us from even standing up (verse 3).

- But God is listening, more than ready to help, to forgive us (verse 4).

- His Word, His faithful promises, are our only hope for rescue (verse 5).

- We strain to see His arrival through our darkness (verse 6).

- We hope in His great love and His overwhelming desire to save us (verse 7).

- He will save us, He promised to come, and then He did come…to Bethlehem (verse 8).

The problem in this story is the ending—the captive is unwilling to be saved. That's the part you play, be willing to be rescued, to repent (change your mind about running away from your Rescuer). You have to give up, surrender, and believe in Jesus' payment for your sins on the cross was enough, that His resurrection proved His bagful of cash was sufficient to bring you home to a heartbroken Father. And that's how Psalm 130 relates…if you want a Merry Christmas.

Appendix II – My Story

Tough Questions

The bedroom door flew open. My oldest brother stood in the doorway sobbing. "Phillip! Wake up. Jack's dead. He's killed himself. He blew himself up in his car with gasoline." I had never before seen my brother cry, but I watched him walk away that night sobbing uncontrollably. Both shocked and sad, I sat there wondering one question…why? Why did my brother Jack kill himself?

After the funeral, still another question haunted me…where was my brother Jack now? The body that we placed in the ground was nothing more than a clay shell. The things that had made Jack a person were no longer there. He was gone. One day he was alive, living in Los Angeles. The next day, I found myself struggling to see his scarred features through a plastic body bag. I realized at that moment just how temporary life really is.

Footsteps

I admired Jack more than anyone else I knew. He was a big, muscular guy---tough with the men and charming with the ladies. He had earned my respect as a fighter in high school, with his "black leather jacket" image and "James Dean" charisma. All through school, I imitated him and followed in his footsteps. Jack was cool and I wanted to be just like him. He seemed to have it totally together…and then he died. What could have made him so hopeless that he'd take his own life? All I had was questions. It wasn't until my freshman year at Michigan State that I finally got some answers.

3 a.m.

It all started with a question that a guy in my dorm asked me one day: "If you died tonight and stood before God, and He asked you why He should let you into His Heaven, what would you say?" It was a pretty heavy question and I was somewhat taken off guard. I wasn't used to being asked such direct questions about God, so I rattled off some "conditioned" response about God's love and forgiveness. But even after I had left his room thinking that I had successfully evaded his question, I couldn't forget it. It dug deep into my conscience. When you experience a death as close as your own brother, you can't help but wonder about God. The reality of death is no longer a "maybe someday." All of a sudden it hits you head on, right in the face!

As the school term wore on, I thought about that guy's question more and more honestly. My brother's death had forced me to realistically evaluate my life, and without excuses. I began to see that I was not "cool," not with God anyway. It really hit me one morning about three o'clock, during a party on our dorm floor. I went down to that guy's room again and woke him up. I was pretty incoherent from partying, as well as scared, but I managed to mumble something about wanting to talk about God. I was scared because I finally admitted to myself for the first time where I thought I was going. No one had to tell me. My life spoke loud and clear.

Once inside the room I told him that I wasn't sure where I would go when I died, but that I wanted to be positive. He still wasn't quite awake, but invited me inside to talk. He showed me a verse in the Bible that said that it was possible to know for certain. "These things I have written to you who believe in the name of the Son of God, in order that you may know that you have eternal life." He explained to me that none of us could naturally be in Heaven with God because He is perfect. No matter how good we have been, we all fall short of God's standard of perfection. That was no news to me. I knew I wasn't perfect---far from it. The Bible calls this condition Sin, which he explained was a Greek archery term for an arrow that had failed to hit the center of the target. But sin is also a very dangerous and lethal thing. Because of it we can't enjoy a relationship with God. "For whoever keeps the whole law and yet stumbles in one point, he has become guilty of all." If we die in this condition of sin, we are not only separated from Him in this life, but for all eternity. "Your sins have made a separation between you and your God."

"...And Justice for All"

Now even though I knew that I wasn't perfect, I had a hard time believing that a loving God would throw me into Hell. One analogy, however, helped me to see that God's character was more than just love. Imagine that I am arrested for drunk driving after losing control of my car and had killed two pedestrians. Later, when my case came up in court, I discovered that the judge was my very own father! Even though my father loves me, as a judge he must punish me to fulfill his duty and obey the law. If he let me off the hook, he would not be just. The families of the people that I had killed would demand justice for my actions. The parallel is clear. Although God loves us, He must punish sin or else He would no longer be righteous. The point is that we are not good enough for a holy God to accept us into Heaven. Our sin cannot be swept under the carpet; it must be dealt with righteously. It was then that I realized that I had a warped concept of God. I had always assumed that when I asked for forgiveness, I got it merely because I asked, but I was never assured of it. How then was I to be forgiven?

God actually became a man, Jesus Christ, in order to satisfy the wrath our sin deserved by dying on the cross. Since God demands a perfect payment for sin, and none of us is perfect, the only one that could pay for our sin was God Himself. "He made Him (Jesus) who knew no sin to become sin on our behalf that we might become the righteousness of God in Him." God's love and justice merged at the cross. But I already believed these things that he was telling me. What was I missing?

Action!

If I told you that I put a rattlesnake in your bed, would you sleep there that night? Of course not if you believed me. Real faith, a real saving-eternal faith, involves action. If you really believe something, then you'll act on it. I realized that though I intellectually agreed with these facts, I had never acted on them. It was simply head knowledge. So that night, I admitted to God that I was a sinner and needed His forgiveness. I freely gave God control of my life and made Him my Lord, promising to follow and obey because of what He had done for me. Even though I had chosen to be indifferent with God, my brother's death forced me to answer some tough questions. What made my brother so hopeless was that he had chosen to ignore Christ's payment for his sin. All he had to hope in was in this life and it never satisfied him. Are you satisfied? I'd like to challenge you to consider today whether or not you're positive that you're going to Heaven. If you're not sure, I'd love to talk to you.

A special thanks to Amy, Leah, Dan, Jeremy, Kailee, Emily, Dale, Patty, and DW. I'm grateful to all of you for your encouragements and taking the time to read my columns before going to press, so I only look dumb (and not sound dumb too).

To Peter for his mule-like efforts to rock out this book's design and edits, Bill and Chris for double-checking me, Ron for his kind words about my words, and above all...

the wild Lion of Judah who mercifully spared me, and then gave me His words. This book is my thank you to You!

Made in the USA
Monee, IL
24 January 2022